SPIRITl
ENTREPRENEURSHIP

Navigating Success with Soul

AUTHORS

Kim Brockway

Louise Baines

Amy Deards

Alison Dee

Samantha Grundy

Rachael Hall

Joanne Lazarus

Judith Rayner

Charlotte Saunders

Table of Contents

Foreword by Anna Parker-Naples

My hands were shaking on the steering wheel, covered in red spots that hadn't been there half an hour before. A glance in the rearview mirror confirmed my cheeks were flushing a beetroot hue, as though I were purging every toxin in my body. I pulled my trusty Kia over to the side of the country road and retched into the grass. Gradually coming back to myself, I sat on the patchy turf and breathed. As if my whole world had been turned upside down. In fact, it had been. I knew nothing would be the same again.

Earlier that afternoon, I had been the recipient of a deep hypnosis and NLP (Neuro-Linguistic Programming) session as part of my certification to become a master practitioner. My mentor and fellow student could see that the process was having a significant impact on me and decided to keep going beyond our allotted time. To say I am glad they did is an understatement. I was transported in my mind to a place beyond.

Beyond what? Earth, our galaxy, the universe? I didn't know, except that a new awareness had landed in me. I was far more than the human body and brain I inhabited. My understanding of myself went beyond my accomplishments and achievements (as a Type A, ambitious, high achiever this realisation was both mind-blowing and a bit ego-shattering). I had a visceral experience of being part of the stars and a tiny fragment of the fabric in between. From this vantage anything was possible. As my conscious mind returned to the present, I felt invigorated, free. Everything in my life shifted from that moment onwards.

No-one can ever tell you that you've had a spiritual awakening. No-one can confirm or deny your deeply personal and profound experience. Whilst there may be commonalities that resonate with others who have woken up to their limitless potential, to their connection to Source, Spirit, the Universe, or God (whichever name for the same concept that speaks to you), they still cannot provide conclusive evidence as to whether you did or did not have an awakening. Only you know, and once it's happened there's no permanent forgetting. Sure, the pressures of day-to-day life may make your mammoth remembering seem more distant, but once you *know* your heart, body, and mind that you have had an encounter with a higher part of yourself, it never leaves you.

Sometimes I'll forget for a while that I am a spiritual being inside a human body as my vehicle, mired down by stressors with my work, at home, with family, friends, all the things. I'll focus more on the practical, the 'getting stuff done', I'll fall into old patterns of striving for achievement and recognition. Until a challenging event occurs that brings me to my knees, that brings me to remembering: I am more than this. Again and again.

You'll hear mention of my Breathwork Academy and BreathHealing Release™ Method throughout this book. These were creative inspirations born out of what has become a direct hotline to my inner wisdom, the spokesman for my higher self. After a particularly challenging period of burnout, I learnt how to breathe deeply, to shut my ears to the external noise and listen to the gentle voice inside me. When I'm tapped into my body, when I'm attuned to the energy that courses around and through me, when I'm alert to the subtleties of messages that are brought to me intuitively I make the right decisions. Right for me at least, even if they defy expectation and logic to the outside world.

As I embrace my own connection to a power greater than myself it fuels me to spread the word, no longer pretending this deeper part of me doesn't exist. There are many reasons I have held back from doing this in the past. Fear of sounding crazy. Fear of judgement. Fear of rejection. I believe these all stem from the genetic 'handing down' of unimaginable terror relating to the witch trials across Europe, and most especially to the Scottish villages of my ancestors over 25 generations ago. Brutality was shown to any woman who went against religious norms, to share her healing gifts and wisdoms, to share that she felt connected to the earth, moon, stars and beyond. Thankfully times are changing, as increasing numbers of people across the globe have awakening experiences and refuse to hide the light of their own spirituality any longer.

In these pages, you'll find how accessing and acknowledging a spiritual connection is the thread that offers trust, hope and inspiration. How following the internal nudges and seemingly unconnected serendipitous moments can cause unique concepts and creations to be formed in the business world. Businesses that serve a greater purpose, that aim for profit (of course), but strive for far beyond financial gain. These businesses, and the women at their helm, deliver from a place of service, for the greater good of others. As you read them, I urge you to tap in and listen to what spiritual messages are stored within your own personal hotline to source (your body). What's the new direction that has been whispering to you for a long while? What's the brave action that's niggling at you, that goes against your usual rational thinking and behaviours? In my experience, that's where the most special and important creations reside, ready to take us to places we never dreamed possible. So, as you read this book with your eyes, I invite you to listen more closely to the answers that rest within you.

Love Anna.

Introduction by Kim Brockway

Dear Reader,

Welcome to *Spiritual Entrepreneurship: Navigating Success With Soul*. This book beautifully captures the essence of soul-led entrepreneurship and growth, and I'm thrilled to present it to you.

I have experienced a journey into the world of entrepreneurship filled with twists, turns, and moments of profound insight. Along the way, I realised that success is not just about financial gain or professional achievements; it's about aligning our work with our deepest values and spiritual truths.

Why did I want to create this book? In today's fast-paced and often chaotic world, we need entrepreneurs who lead with heart and soul. Successful business owners know that making a difference in people's lives is more important than just making money. I have had the privilege of meeting such individuals. I wanted to shine a spotlight on female entrepreneurs who embrace spirituality, compassion, and authenticity in their businesses.

Spiritual Entrepreneurship is a testament to the power of blending business acumen with spiritual wisdom. Within these pages, you'll discover stories of resilience, courage, and transformation. Explore the journeys of entrepreneurs who built businesses with purpose and passion. Learn how they overcame challenges and embraced their true selves.

My vision for this book is simple: to encourage and empower aspiring entrepreneurs on their own spiritual journey. Regardless of your level of experience, I hope the stories in this book illuminate your path and remind you of your unlimited potential.

As we celebrate the spring, a time of renewal and new beginnings, I invite you to join us on this journey of self-discovery, growth, and transformation. Together, let's plant the seeds of change and cultivate a world where business is not just a means of making a living, but a vehicle for making a difference.

With love and thanks,

Kim Brockway

Editor, *Spiritual Entrepreneurship: Navigating Success With Soul*

April 2024

Chapter One

Alison Dee

"Trust the process. Your time will come" ~ *Unknown.*

Listening to My Intuition

It's so noisy in the online space, and it truly messed with my head for a long time. I tried following all the experts' advice, and it only led me to burnout.

So I took a step back, tapped into my intuition and started doing what felt *right ... eventually.*

I've had quite a journey into entrepreneurship and I'm going to tell you everything I wish I'd known when I was just starting out. Just maybe I'll save you several years of going round in circles because you'll learn to shut out the noise much easier, and tune into yourself (and what you need) much earlier on.

I've second guessed myself more times than I can count and honestly — while I can give you all the guidance in the world — the most important thing I can say to you is that there isn't ever only one way of doing things. If you have an idea, then research it, look into the logistics of it, and find a way to make it work — you were given the idea for a reason. All the time I'm finding different people who are doing different things and making it work for them and it's always giving me new ideas. Nail your marketing and your messaging (and be authentic and have integrity) and it will work.

From Multi-Level Marketing (MLM) to Life Coaching

I have wanted my own business for a very long time, but after a few failed attempts in MLM (sometimes called Network Marketing) because of struggling with following their rules and always being harassed to hit targets, I decided to focus on a 'career' instead.

So, my life coaching story begins in 2019 when I'd just qualified and registered as a biomedical scientist — the 'career'. After being forced back into study after a decade away from it (I needed to repeat my final year to get the honours to my biomedical science degree), I really found my love for it. I was super keen to start on the next step, which was my specialist portfolio, but I became embroiled in lab politics (thanks Universe!) and I was blocked from doing it. Desperate to seek another outlet I came across an online diploma in mindfulness and I was intrigued. It was only around £15, but I kept getting pop ups to upgrade to a diploma in mindfulness and life coaching. I felt so pulled towards it, even though at about £29 it felt like such an enormous investment to me. That was definitely the start of my journey into life coaching. Despite my years of interest in personal development, I quickly realised I had I barely begun to explore its depths. I realised coaching ticked all the boxes for me. MLM was a struggle for me because selling products didn't bring me fulfilment. I didn't feel like I was making a real tangible difference to someone's life. With life coaching, however, I could really make an impact and that felt so empowering and motivating.

Trial by Fire: Manipulation, Lessons, and Resilience

Alongside this I came across a coach online who I'd been following for a while and she had a free challenge that I signed up to (having no idea how these things worked).

To be completely blunt, I was totally manipulated into signing up for her programme. First she announced it as being £1000, which soon changed to £2000 after I showed interest. She absolutely harassed me, leaving me google voicemails shaming me into signing up, and I just felt like I could not say no. She promised me I'd earn the money back in six weeks, so despite my financial concerns, she suggested a deposit. Her six-week course was not as robust as I was expecting.

I ended up taking out a loan to pay for it. She congratulated me on doing so, saying I'd 'activated my warrior' by doing that. She showed me no compassion and challenged my emotional security so much it took me to the brink of a mental meltdown. I felt like everything was falling apart and I didn't know what to believe or trust anymore.

With her guidance, I set up a Facebook group and put together a 6-week course. Which totally flopped because I did not know how to launch it (I didn't even know what 'launching' meant).

So the six weeks of her course ended, and I was left with a Facebook group like a ghost town, a course structure I didn't have any faith in, and zero belief in myself as a coach. I felt completely lost and started investigating coaching certifications. She told me I was only looking to get a certification because I thought others would judge me. She said that she was doing great with no certifications (*hmmmm…*) but I knew deep down that this was important to me. I felt so conflicted - it really left me questioning myself. I eventually realised it wasn't the certification that was important but the *training* that went with it - so that I could show up with confidence and actually understand how to create results for my clients.

It took me quite a while to get over this experience and I didn't learn all the lessons straight away. But on reflection, it made me realise a lot about who I wanted to be. It cemented the kind of coach I wanted to show up as and the way I wanted to treat people.

Life's Turmoil: Navigating Loss and Workplace Challenges

I had been following the Clique Academy for a few months and it felt really aligned to me, but after my very recent coaching disaster I was super wary and cautious.

For the first time in my life, I felt like I was at a crossroads, with a decision to make that would change the entire trajectory of my life. I was procrastinating on making a decision and then I had to have my beloved cat, Gizmo, put to sleep. I was absolutely devastated and my work was entirely unsympathetic.

It made me realise I really really didn't want to be beholden to a 'boss' for the rest of my working life — I wanted choices, I wanted freedom and I wanted to be able to prioritise myself. Life Coaching was my ticket to getting out of employment and so I made the decision to go for it.

My parents didn't like the idea, and my partner didn't really understand it, so I felt like not only did I have no support, but that I was going against the grain. I've never done that in my life because I was such a people pleaser. But the second I was signed up, and it was all finalised I had the most overwhelming sense of relief — and I'm still so glad to this day that I signed up.

I had such a strong '*why*'. I'd come in after a manic day in the lab (this was just when the pandemic started). Then I'd study, or I'd hop on to a live in my Facebook group. Daily life in the lab gave me an awful lot of content and I was completely full of inspiration. It took me just four months to power through my coaching certification and I was absolutely on top of the world with it.

Just showing up daily was enough for me — to share my life lessons and getting the interaction back was what I lived for. I ran a couple of challenges and attempted to 'launch' some coaching programmes, but they totally flopped. I realised I still wasn't getting the business side of things.

Then I had the idea to start a membership. I brainstormed with a few people and got feedback. They told me to charge £111 a month for what I was offering. It seemed exciting, but then I had a reality check. Why would I expect others to pay that much when I wouldn't? Then I reduced the fee to £89, but that still seemed ridiculous to me, so eventually I settled on £39 a month. I did a 'soft launch' and got ten members straight away. I absolutely loved it — I was in my element and my members were responding so well to everything I put out. However, over the next year or so, I really struggled to grow my membership — I just didn't feel aligned to the price I'd set. I got caught up in the excitement of it, but when the day-to-day reality hit, it didn't feel right and the energy was off. Then everything started going wrong.

Rock Bottom: Re-evaluating Priorities

I was actually in the final stages of burnout. It didn't occur to me then. I hadn't processed the emotions from losing my cat (and my godmother a week later) and I'd just thrown myself into my coaching business without pausing for breath.

The first thing that happened was I got a catfish in the membership who was not who he said he was, and he completely changed the dynamic. He was masquerading as someone who was interested in personal development. In reality, he was a predator — catfish are people who pretend to be something other than they are to trick people.

My members weren't showing up for the calls anymore and it was awkward. In hindsight, I know my intuition was screaming at me that this was wrong, but I was so focused on helping and pleasing everyone, I totally ignored it. Eventually, I told him he'd have to leave the membership and refunded him. He tried making me feel guilty, but then I found out about his past and realised what a shady character he was. Although I regret not acting sooner, I'm glad I did finally act.

If you're worried about catfishing, here are some tips:

- Check them out and listen to your intuition

- Don't give out personal information

- Don't be afraid to ask questions - anyone genuine won't mind answering them

- Look for any holes in their stories - it'll be obvious if things don't add up

The second thing that happened was my cat went missing (after I lost Gizmo, I was lucky enough to get Poppet and then Stripe). Stripe was only one-year-old and still such a little cat. My partner and I spent two days walking the streets, calling for her and not sleeping at all. We were beside ourselves and couldn't stop fearing the worst. Luckily, after putting flyers through neighbours' doors, we were alerted to her being just a few doors down and stuck up a tree!! Thank goodness my partner's tall and could get her down!

And then the third and final thing — the subtle bullying and harassment I'd been suffering from my line manager in the lab hit an absolute peak. I had the worst anxiety attack I've ever had and got signed off ill with stress.

I was in functional burnout before these things, but the added stress of them pushed me into the final stages of burnout and I couldn't cope anymore. Everything suffered and while I was off ill (for four months) I had to step away from posting because obviously I couldn't be seen to still be building a business while I was off ill.

Despite having more to learn and no income strategy, I chose to quit my job. I was so angry, and I felt like I'd been completely failed.

Rising from the Ashes: Lessons in Manifestation and Boundaries

I threw myself into a launch straight away and, of course, it didn't do very well — I'd neglected my audience for about five months and had no build up time. It completely knocked my confidence, and I didn't launch again for seven months. By this point I'd learnt a lot about visibility and although the next launch didn't go great, I knew I hadn't been very visible so I straight away launched again with a focus on being so much more visible and it worked!! That launch went so much better.

And then ... I went back into my shell again. Thoughts of my business consumed me, but I wasn't actually really showing up, being very visible or productive. I'd sit and scroll through social media all day, but I wasn't posting or really even networking with anyone — I was in pure procrastination mode.

I made a new friend online and thought I'd found my new bestie. She seemed to totally get me, and as my defences were pretty low after everything I'd been through, I wasn't being very vigilant. She quickly took over my life, messaging me from 7am to midnight and getting narky when I wasn't replying. My partner, whom I've been with for a long time, even made her resentful.

At first I welcomed the interaction — after all, I was at home all day and I was pretty lonely — but eventually I realised how toxic she was. I tried to distance myself from her and she got really nasty and abusive. Although that's not the first time I've experienced that, hopefully I've now learnt from it. Because of those repeated lessons, I have not experienced anyone treating me that way for the past two years. I've set my boundaries and listen to my intuition, so I just don't attract people like that anymore.

So I decided to get a job. But for all the wrong reasons. I felt like I'd drawn the short straw. My pride was not happy with me and my energy was totally in the wrong place. Which is why it took nearly three months for me to find something (and it was temporary). While initially the job seemed great, it quickly fell apart — thankfully within three months I was being let go. Initially, I was happy to be free, but then reality hit. With the 'security' of this job, I'd wound my business down so I could rebrand and refocus. Now suddenly I had to make it work again. I made knee jerk decisions and threw myself back into it, but imposter syndrome quickly threw me into inertia and the scroll hole once more.

I had the absolute fear that I couldn't pay my bills, and that froze me into inaction. My nervous system was completely out of whack and I wasn't sleeping, meaning I was spending my days in bed absolutely exhausted. I'd hit rock bottom, and I felt so conflicted and overwhelmed. How could I show up as a life coach when my entire life felt like it was such a mess? Somehow I was getting by, but this wasn't living, it was surviving. I was *just* managing to get by every month and it felt life was such a shambles.

I knew something had to give. Something had to change, and I just wasn't in a place to show up for my business. Plus, I was bored; I was lonely, and I just wasn't enjoying life. Entrepreneurship wasn't living up to the vision I had in my head. I didn't have freedom — I was completely trapped by my situation and I felt utterly desolate.

Rediscovering Confidence and Clarity

And that's when I decided my pride had a lot to answer for. It was keeping me stuck and not being helpful. I thought of what I *needed* - a stable income, to be around people and to have structure. A job would give me all those. So I went on the job search again. This time from the *right* energy and wouldn't you know it, within two days I'd got a temporary position. Within a week, I had an interview for a permanent role, which I started the week after. In that position, I had the opportunity to work with incredible people, which gave me the structure I craved and allowed me to relax.

It took months for my nervous system to get back into balance and for me to start making headway with my finances. But taking a step back from my business gave me clarity. I rebranded as 'The Life Improvement Coach' and protected my business with a trademark. I sat and looked at the offerings I wanted to put out there that were aligned with me.

At the point of writing this chapter, 1:1 coaching isn't really on my agenda. Although I wouldn't turn it down if anyone approached me, it's not something I want to actively market. I am focusing on group coaching and mentoring - which is easier to scale and protects my energy more efficiently and effectively. I've learnt what suits me and what I feel most comfortable with. Even though it's different from what most people suggest and offer in the industry, it works for me. I feel like I finally have confidence in myself and my abilities. I *know* how to move forward. Instead of just hoping, I have a clear vision and strategy which takes so much pressure off.

Vision + Strategy + Energy = Manifesting Results

You can get results purely from strategy and vision, but when you add the right energy into the mix, it's going to skyrocket your results.

1.   Vision comes first because you can't create a plan and strategy without knowing where you're going and what you want to achieve.

2.   Then you create your strategy so when you actually get in your vehicle you know *how* you're going to get to your destination, and then you bring the energy so it's like you've put rocket fuel in your car.

3.   Finally, create the energy by good old-fashioned mindset work. Create a vision board, do positive affirmations or gratitude daily. Believe in yourself and surround yourself with like-minded people.

Key Insights for Thriving in Entrepreneurship

In the culmination of my journey as an entrepreneur, I've gathered a wealth of insights and lessons that I'm eager to pass on to you. These lessons result from many years of learning, personal growth, and thoughtful reflections on how to navigate the entrepreneurial world with integrity, purpose, and resilience. Embrace the wisdom in these lessons with an open mind:

Lesson 1: Don't Promise What You Can't Guarantee You Can Deliver

Never promise that anyone will make a certain amount of money after working with you. You can share clients' results — but always have a disclaimer. 'This isn't guaranteed'.

Lesson 2: Only Do Something And Let Others Do Something Because It Feels Good And Expansive

Never use manipulation tactics to get someone to sign up to your programme. If they're not ready, they either won't do the work, won't get the results or will be so needy you'll regret taking them on — it's a lose-lose for everyone concerned.

Lesson 3: Never Manipulate Someone Into Getting Into Debt To Sign Up With You

Now, I'm not saying credit cards and loans are bad. It's up to any individual to decide how to manage their finances, and if they *choose* to pay on a credit card/take out a loan, that is entirely on them. It is not up to you to suggest that or manipulate anyone into that. If it's not their decision, the energy exchange will be absolutely awful. They'll be so worried about their debt they won't show up for whatever it is they've paid for. Plus, it's a really shitty thing to do. Just don't do it.

Lesson 4: Credibility Is Important

What does credibility actually mean? It's the quality of being trusted and believed in, and this is so important for the longevity of your business. I knew someone who was an absolutely fantastic marketer but failed to get results for her clients. Despite making

£100k, she'd exhausted her network and had a terrible reputation, so wasn't getting any repeat clients. She returned to her beauty business.

Lesson 5: It Is Important To Have A Constant Flow Of New Followers Coming Through.

There's two parts to a sustainable, expanding business — sell existing products to new people, and sell new products to existing people. You want to create raving fans who consistently buy from you, and recommend you, so you also sell to new people. Do this by setting expectations. Don't promise what you can't deliver. Promise what you can deliver and then over deliver. Be able to back up your claims, whether with qualifications or results, and be consistent.

Lesson 6: Reconnect To Your Why Every Day, Otherwise You'll Lose Sight Of It

This is so important as a business owner. It takes a lot of courage and energy to want to step into entrepreneurship. You have to have an enormous driving force to keep you showing up every day when the going gets tough. So take the time to figure out exactly what your 'why' is and 'why' you want it. Then reconnect to it every single day to keep you motivated and driven.

Lesson 7: Pricing Is An Energy Exchange

I absolutely hate the phrase 'charge your worth', because I've seen many inexperienced, unqualified coaches use it to justify sky-high prices that have no actual results. First, you aren't going to build an excellent reputation that way. Second, it will not feel good (unless you don't care about your clients at all — in which case, why are you a coach?). Prices can always change, and it's far easier to put your prices up than it is to reduce them. Pick a price that feels good — for example getting paid for the value of your time and expertise, and that your client is getting a fair deal with what they get out of it. Reevaluate often and amend your pricing when it feels necessary. If you don't have experience, don't feel bad charging lower — charge what feels valuable to you and your client. You can also market something as a 'beta' price. Offering a lower price may be a strategy to get testimonials and still feel confident in your pricing.

Lesson 8: Don't Take On Any Client — Take On The Ones That Have The Energy You Want To Work With.

I was so desperate to help everyone I didn't think about protecting my energy and it had major consequences. The Universe then threw another lesson at me. I attracted someone who practically became my stalker, who totally trampled over my boundaries and wouldn't leave me alone. Thankfully, I've had my filters on since. I've been strict with my boundaries and I'd say it's been at least two years now since I've had any issues, but DO NOT IGNORE the red flags. If something doesn't feel right, it isn't right. I live by that rule now, quite happily saying no to things that give me that twinge in my gut.

Lesson 9: The Right Time To Leave Your Paid Employment.

I was so unhappy at work. My line manager was bullying me and I was so overworked that I felt completely exhausted. So I gambled on my business, but because I didn't know the action to take and I had no strategy in place, I spent two years living on my nerves, struggling to make ends meet because I was trying to create from a place of panic and lack, which wasn't aligned. We all need stability and security — so create that for yourself. Being self-employed and having all that freedom sounds like a dream. But when you have no money to pay your bills, let alone enjoy yourself, it quickly becomes a nightmare, and then you'll start resenting your business.

Lesson 10: Manifesting Is A Scientific Practice

Yes, really! There is so much science that backs it up, and as a very logical, qualified scientist, that's right up my street. But I really bought into the 'jump and the Universe will catch you' philosophy and that doesn't work without you taking aligned, inspired action. Things don't just fall into your lap if you aren't taking the slightest bit of action. I'm absolutely not saying things can't be easy, because they can, but you have to be taking some sort of action. You also can't manifest your dreams, desires, and goals if you're in a negative mindset, because not only does that affect the action you do or don't take, it also affects your energy and vibration.

Lesson 11: Setting Boundaries Means Everyone Gets The Best Of You, Not The Rest Of You.

This took me a very long time to learn and I admit 'boundaries' is something I still have to work on daily. When you are a heart-led spiritual entrepreneur, you want to show up to serve. That's admirable. *But* not having clear boundaries is one of the fastest ways to burnout, and it's not fun. You are not serving your clients and audience by being so available, because then they come to rely on you. In reality, you want them to be solving their own problems (following your guidance, of course). Protecting your boundaries protects your energy and stops you from falling into the trap of losing yourself in your business. My advice? Set working hours that are non-negotiable (unless there's a deadline or exceptional circumstances). Have notifications switched off; especially on social media, and schedule downtime on your phone so it reminds you've finished work and need to down tools. Also, make sure you plan in fun and social activities so your life doesn't become all business. Especially at the beginning, when it's all exciting, shiny and new and you just want to spend all your time in your business. When you have clear boundaries from the outset, they are far easier to enforce. Your audience and clients will never expect more from you because you've set those clear expectations.

Lesson 12: Don't Let Pride Get In The Way

If it's right for you, you'll find people will be more supportive than you ever thought. Usually, the 'pride' that's holding us back is something we've created in our own heads that isn't even really a thing.

Lesson 13: Protect Your Nervous System At All Costs

This is the big one I've heard no-one else talk about. When you are struggling to the point you have financial worries, you are challenging your most basic physiological and safety needs. This will put your nervous system completely out of sync. You will not be sleeping properly, you'll under- or over-eat and you will be irritable and withdrawn. It's a terrible place to be. The biggest thing that will suffer (other than yourself) is your business. You won't feel inspired, you won't feel like showing up and being visible, and imposter syndrome will be extremely prevalent. It is absolutely not worth it in my experience.

Lesson 14: Create From Abundance And Expansion, Not Panic, Frustration, And Shortage

Which leads me nicely on to this. When you take care of your nervous system and focus on your mindset, you can create from a place of abundance and expansion. It is a truly wonderful place to be. This is where it feels like everything manifests effortlessly and it's just a dream. So take the time to prioritise you and your energy. It's worth taking a month out to be able to create your business from this space.

Lesson 15: I Realised My True Values

It's easy to fall into the trap of thinking you want what everyone else is parading around. I said my values were 'Freedom, Fun and Fulfilment', and don't get me wrong — those are still very important to me, but after losing the security of my monthly income, I realised my top values are stability and security.

Lesson 16: *You* Are The Only Person Who Puts Pressure On Yourself To Succeed.

Make sure it's the right pressure from a place of intuition, abundance, and creativity — not frustration and negativity and judgement.

Lesson 17: Why Wouldn't You Create From Abundance And Expansion?

Because of self-imposed goals and deadlines? Why not let everything flow just as it's meant to? Why try to force it and race ahead? As someone with Attention Deficit Hyperactivity Disorder

(ADHD) I am the absolute worst for this, but when I sit back and allow, it's amazing how the energy flows. When I impose deadlines for no reason other than my own impatience, it creates such resistance energy I get blocked. So, if you're feeling blocked, why not do a meditation, sit back and release, and see how that feels — you might be surprised at what comes up.

Lesson 18: Perspective

When you see others giving advice and guidance, they're showing you their highlight reel, not behind-the-scenes — where the struggle really happened. I do get a little baffled sometimes at how people just make it sound easy. Because I've never known anyone really, truly has it that easy. They just want to make themselves sound better, so they miss out on the hard bits — meanwhile you're left wondering why you can't do what they did. Every overnight success has years of struggle behind them. Plus, you are on your own journey and no-one else is you — embrace your own journey and only look to others' successes to motivate and inspire you.

Lesson 19: What Worked For Others May Not Work For You.

Try to see but detach from the outcome — it doesn't mean anything about you. Having your own business is a constant cycle of experimentation, rinse and repeat. You find what works for you, and you do it again, but maybe bigger and better. You find what doesn't work for you and chalk it up to experience — maybe it needs a tweak or even a total rework, or maybe you never speak of it again. All business is a numbers game. While you may be soul-led, what gets you getting back up time and time again is taking a step back, detaching emotionally and crunching those numbers. I did a launch where I didn't sell anything; when I analysed it, I'd barely been visible (even though it had consumed my headspace), so I relaunched a month later and sold several spots because I was so much more visible.

Lesson 20: Give Value And Let People Get To Know You.

That's literally it. The more people can see of you, the more they get to know, like, and trust you. When people know, like, and trust you, they will come to you — sales will feel effortless and fulfilling — you won't feel like you need to 'sell'.

Don't get me wrong, I have had some truly amazing moments in my business where I can't quite believe it's happening to me! I've been on the sales team for a seven-figure launch (picked out of 120 people), been on countless podcasts and delivered many training sessions. I have got to know some absolutely incredible people who I speak to daily.

I've been on a massive personal development journey, learning boundaries and what I *do* want, and this greatly influences how I present my offerings. I've learnt to tune into myself and if it doesn't feel right, I question it and refocus until it becomes aligned. The biggest thing I've learnt is to work with a strategic plan, instead of relying on hope and luck.

A trained, certified coach, NLP Master Practitioner, and published author, I am also a qualified biomedical scientist so I put the 'woo' and science together.

I am passionate about helping those new to personal development understand the logical steps they can take to start creating their dreams.

I am an expert at finding the lessons, positives, and gratitude in any situation — a far cry from the negative, conflicted 'glass half empty' person I used to be!

Living in Coventry, UK with my partner Jason and two cats; Poppet and Stripe, I am happiest when out in nature, usually with a glass of red wine.

Meet Alison Dee

Alison Dee is a qualified life coach and NLP Master Practitioner with a profound commitment to empowering professional women to live authentically and in alignment with their values. With a background in biomedical science, Alison's own entrepreneurial journey is a testament to the transformative power of self-awareness and strategic action in the business world.

Having navigated a series of personal and professional challenges, including overcoming manipulative business practices and personal loss, Alison has developed a coaching philosophy centred on integrity, resilience, and authenticity. Her personal experiences deeply informed her approach, from her initial struggles with conventional career paths and the pressures of societal expectations, to her ultimate realisation of the importance of internal validation and self-guided decision-making.

Alison, a skilled coach, uses mindfulness, life coaching and holistic techniques to help clients overcome societal pressures and achieve personal and professional growth. Her work involves guiding women to achieve self-fulfilment by aligning their professional aspirations with their personal values.

Alison's credentials include; Diplomas in Mindfulness, EFT, and the Law of Attraction, a Life Coach certification and Money Mindset certification from the International Coaching Federation (ICF) Accredited Clique Academy, and an NLP Master Practitioner certificate from the Centre of Excellence. She is currently advancing her qualifications with further certifications in life coaching and NLP.

The Dee-Lightful Living® Club, founded by Alison, helps women gain confidence and empowerment through life coaching. In 2021 she also founded the Positive Mindset Tribe®, a free group that helps anyone learn about how the power of positive mindset can help them not only improve their lives but also improve their mental health and she is so passionate about making this a worldwide brand to give people the resources to help themselves. She is also a published author and a passionate advocate for creating a balanced life that honours one's inner voice and personal vision.

LINKS

Facebook: https://www.facebook.com/AlisonDeeCoaching

Instagram: https://www.instagram.com/i_am_alisondee

Website: https://www.dee-lightfulliving.com/

Chapter Two

Amy Deards

The hustle, the decisions, the endless to-do lists of normal day-to-day life as an entrepreneur—it is like a whirlwind, right? We make endless plans, set goal after goal, create strategy after strategy, often with a blind hope that this time it will work. But what if there was a secret sauce? A power that goes beyond the strategies, blending the every day with something deeper? Want to know the secret that has been a game-changer for me in this rollercoaster called business? And it is not your typical plan or a killer marketing strategy, either. It is something far more magical and personal.

I am not your usual mindset and confidence coach — I am the one who is fighting a never-ending war. Do not get me wrong, I am winning all the battles so far. I guess you could say I have made it through the dark and into the light, with a pocketful of wisdom and a dash of spirituality. So, I hope you join me as I open the door to a dimension rarely explored in the business world — a space where intuition becomes a compass, recovery is a testament to resilience, and a higher power lights the path to empowerment.

In this chapter, I invite you to step into the inner workings of not just my business, but my often-crazy mind, my soul, and the mysterious magic that shows up in my life, just when I need it the most. You have got your very own backstage pass to the behind-the-scenes of my entrepreneurial success.

I have discovered that in the chaos of business, there is a rhythm; It is the rhythm of intuition, recovery, and a sprinkle of something higher guiding the way. This is not your typical business tale; it is a story of how spirituality became my surprising sidekick in this amazing adventure.

So, grab a cup of coffee, get cosy, and let us dive into the unspoken magic that happens when you blend the practical with the profound. This is a space where gut feelings are trusted, recovery becomes a superpower, and spirituality is not just a buzzword — it is the secret weapon that turns the ordinary into the extraordinary. This is not just my story; it is an open invitation for you to explore the uncharted territories of entrepreneurship with a sprinkle of spiritual stardust. Now, who does not want that?

Let's rewind to May 2019, a crucial moment that would shape everything ahead. Picture this: it's a lovely May morning at 11 am. The sun is beaming, casting a warm glow through the curtains, and suddenly, there's a loud banging at my door. For a moment, confusion clouds my thoughts, but then the realisation hits. My memory, a rare occurrence after three years of heavy alcohol use that often left me in a blackout haze, suddenly returned. I could manage daily tasks, even work, but usually, I had no recollection of how I spent my time. However, on that particular day, everything became clear — it was the day I chose to enter rehab.

I was well aware of my alcohol problem, and that awareness lingered for quite some time. However, putting into words the sheer terror of letting go of the one thing that seemed to anchor me in the chaos of my life was challenging. It wasn't normal to wake up needing a drink to steady my hands, but that had become my reality. My days were a blur of boxed wine, occasional cocaine binges, casual encounters, and an un-fillable void within me, no matter how hard I tried.

I desperately yearned for it to stop, but here's the catch that many don't grasp about addicts — we genuinely don't know how to stop. I had no clue how regular people managed without a drink or ten at the beginning or end of the day. Yet desperation, strange as it may sound, turned out to be a profound blessing. It guided me to the ultimate turning point in my life-rock bottom.

So, there I was, perched on the windowsill, cigarette in one hand, a glass of wine in the other, watching my mum pack my bags because a spot had been secured at a facility sixty miles away. To say fear consumed me would be an understatement. If I'm honest, I didn't want to go. In my mind, life wasn't that bad. But the guilt of my parents spending thousands for my much-needed help pushed me through those doors, almost stumbling.

I had convinced myself that the next 28 days would be a bit of a break, a chance to drink more normally, and life would magically turn rosy. Oh, how wrong I was because in rehab, there's no hiding. Every person there, from the woman at reception to the therapist giving me a reality check, is battling their own addiction. Life got real, fast.

No easing in. No gentle start because detox was on the agenda. From day one, they probed to reveal the truth of who you are, what you're doing. But here's the thing — it's not just about exposing the struggles; it's about unveiling the potential of who you can become.

For years I found myself trapped in a life I no longer recognised — a version of myself buried beneath the weight of despair, anxiety, and the haunting of my past struggles. Mornings were met with disappointment rather than hope, and the very act of existing felt like a heavy burden. But, within that darkness, a spark ignited.

The concept of a higher power is well known in recovery circles. I did not get it. I had secretly admired people who had a blind faith in the divine, but how did they find it? "You do not have to believe in God, you just need to believe that just for today, you are being looked after." Those were the words spoken to me one morning in rehab, and it all made sense. If I was not being looked after, then I simply would not be here. So, if I was being looked after, what was it all for? There had to be reason, an explanation, a purpose to my life.

I no longer wanted to be this pitiful, depressed, anxious shell of a human who just existed. I yearned to reclaim the old Amy—the one who chased happiness, pursued dreams, and transformed challenges into success. More than anything, I aspired to be part of that rare 4%, the warriors who emerge victorious in the first year of sobriety.

So, with a heart full of determination, I set my sights on a goal — a goal that would redefine not only my life but the course of my journey toward recovery and success. It was time to let spirituality be my compass.

From Surrender to Entrepreneurship: Navigating the Unseen Path

In the unpredictable nature of recovery, my initial goal was not to launch a business — it was simply to stay sober. A straightforward aim, yet it presented challenges that showed up in every corner of life. Triggers lurked everywhere, from family disputes to sunny pub garden afternoons, and the constant threat of temptations at social events. Boundaries became my lifeline, particularly with me.

Yet, amid the chaos, a silent force emerged—one that could not be seen or touched but could unquestionably be felt. This invisible power guided my steps and urged me to make choices aligned with a path of recovery. Early on, I accepted a profound truth: my best thinking had led me to rehab, so I had to surrender. Surrender not just to sobriety, but to the notion that I did not always know what was best for me.

Recovery demanded a radical shift in perspective. My ego revealed itself as an internal force fuelled by fear — the same fear that had shadowed my every step. Fear of failure, rejection, and perpetually falling short haunted me. Alcohol, my supposed solution, only magnified these fears, pushing people away and keeping me trapped in isolation.

The turning point came with a choice — to continue down a path of fear or embrace a different journey guided by faith. In surrendering my ego, my fears, and all that lay beyond my control to a force I could not see, touch, but undeniably feel, I found a huge sense of freedom.

And so the seeds of entrepreneurship were planted in the soil of surrender. By relinquishing the need for control and embracing the guidance of a force beyond myself, I discovered an uncharted path that led to the birth of my own business.

The Birth of a Business with Spiritual Roots

In letting go of control and surrendering to something bigger than myself, a whole new vision unfolded. It went beyond just staying sober — it embraced a life driven by purpose and making a positive impact. This shift redefined my whole life. Sharing my journey became more than a just a tool to keep me well — it turned into a tool for sharing the lessons of surrender and resilience with others on their own journeys.

Confession time: The moment I spilled the beans about my recovery on the vast stage of Facebook, I was terrified. Fear of judgement kept me silent me for a whopping sixteen months, but deep down, I knew I could not keep living a façade. After spending decades in the shadows, nearly letting those secrets be my undoing, I refused to repeat the same mistake on my journey of sobriety.

This pivotal decision was not just a personal revelation — it became the spark that ignited my venture into entrepreneurship. As I laid bare my experiences, I found a flood of people reaching out, not just about addiction, but intrigued by the workings of my mindset. They wanted to know the secrets. How did I pull off such a rapid life transformation? How did I morph into this upgraded version of myself?

It hit me — I could teach them. And that marked the beginning of something extraordinary.

My business is not just about making money; it is a living example of the strength found in vulnerability and the ability to adapt. The vision was not just a plan; it was an invitation for others to discover the power of surrender in their lives. My whole mission became one of emphasising honesty, authenticity, and a commitment to growth.

Surrender Isn't Defeat; It's a Doorway to New Possibilities. My Business Became a Testament to the Transformative Power of Surrender.

The business is not solely focused on personal success; it aims to create a positive impact. It became a platform for helping others in their journeys of healing and self-discovery. Through coaching, mentorship, and sharing stories, I became a source of inspiration for those seeking a life free from fear and their own self-imposed limitations.

In simple terms, surrendering opened the door to a bigger story — one where business success is tied to making a difference in the lives of others. The business, born from personal surrender, now stands as proof of the incredible possibilities that unfold when we let go and follow a path guided by something greater. It is not just a business; it is a living example of the transformative journey that happens when you surrender to a higher purpose.

Making Guided Decisions: Navigating Business with Intuition and Purpose

In the ever-shifting world of business, the journey from surrender to entrepreneurship became a story of making guided decisions — choices infused with intuition and purpose. As I embraced the power of surrender, it wasn't just about letting go of control; it was about leaning into a deeper wisdom that transcended the visible. This shift in approach became the heartbeat of my business, influencing every decision, every strategy, and every interaction.

In the throes of recovery, I discovered the magic of intuition — the quiet whispers that guided me toward the right path. As I transitioned into the realm of business, this intuitive guidance seamlessly transformed into a compass for decision-making. It wasn't about blindly following gut feelings; it was about tapping into a source of wisdom that often eludes logical thinking.

Just As Intuition Guided Me Through Recovery, It Now Shapes Every Move in My Business. Trusting That Inner Compass Has Become My Secret Weapon in Decision-making.

Decisions in business often come with the pressure to be logical, data-driven, and objective. However, my journey of surrender taught me the value of balancing logic with intuition. It isn't about dismissing facts; it is about integrating the tangible with the intangible — acknowledging that sometimes, the most profound decisions are felt before they are fully understood. Logic is crucial, but don't ignore the subtle nudges of intuition. The sweet spot lies in finding the balance between the two.

Picture it as a dance with the unseen currents beneath the surface. Just as recovery taught me to navigate the hidden depths of my emotions, making guided decisions in business involves sensing the opportunities and challenges that may not be immediately apparent. It's about embracing the unknown and trusting that there's wisdom beyond what the eyes can perceive. Not every opportunity is visible on the surface. Sometimes, the best decisions come from navigating the unseen currents with intuition as your guide.

Surrendering wasn't a one-time event, though. It is a continuous journey. Making guided decisions in business becomes a natural continuation of that surrender. It means acknowledging that I can't control every outcome, but I can work through the twists and turns with a blend of logic and intuition.

Every decision I make carries the weight of authenticity — a lesson I learnt in surrender. It isn't just about what makes strategic sense; it is about what resonates with my core values. Guided decisions, in essence, are decisions aligned with truth.

Being authentic isn't just a trendy term; it's the North Star in my decision-making process. The moment I start trying to be someone I'm not, comparing myself to others, or making decisions that don't align with my core values, it triggers an imposter syndrome. It feels like I'm playing a role, waiting to be exposed. I played this game for too many years during my active addiction and continuing it in my sobriety was not an option. I've learnt that staying true to myself is non-negotiable; it's the foundation for everything else in my life to work.

It boils down to a deep belief that when I stay true to who I am, decisions naturally fall into place, guiding me toward where I'm meant to be. It's not just about authenticity; it's about creating a path where decisions align with my truth, making the journey smoother and, more often than not, leading me to the right destination.

But there's another piece to this puzzle, a quality that has been both my anchor in recovery and a secret weapon in business — vulnerability. Now, vulnerability might not be the first word that comes to mind when thinking about business success, but in my journey, I've discovered its transformative power.

Embracing Vulnerability: A Source of Strength in Recovery and Business

In the world of recovery, authenticity means shedding the layers of pretence and letting the true self emerge. It's a similar thing in business, where authenticity is not just about showcasing strengths, but also embracing vulnerability. The willingness to be open about challenges, uncertainties, and the occasional stumble has been a game-changer. Just as I learnt in recovery, being real in business means embracing vulnerability. It's not about being flawless; it's about being genuine, and that includes showing the raw, unpolished edges.

In a world that often glorifies strength as an absence of weakness, I know that true strength lies in showing vulnerability; admitting when I don't have all the answers or when I've made a mistake isn't a sign of weakness — It's a display of strength. I am well known among my community for being honest, for being authentic, and telling things the way that they are. Vulnerability became my bridge to connection. My audience no longer felt alone in their struggles. Through my raw emotion, I give them permission to allow themselves some grace and to know that not knowing all the answers doesn't mean they aren't good enough. It allows them to believe in the possibility that they are already good enough, just as they are.

Mistakes Are Part of the Journey. By Openly Learning from Them, We Not Only Grow Individually but Also Cultivate a Mindset of Adaptability and Improvement.

Sharing my journey, being open about the challenges, and revealing the lessons I learn has fostered a sense of trust among clients and followers alike. Vulnerability became the glue that bonded our relationships. I not only connect with others on a human level, but also lay the foundation for trust in my ability to coach and mentor them.

Essentially, my community knows that they are completely accepted. By bringing this principle into my business, it means we are creating a culture where vulnerability is not just okay but valued. It's about creating an environment where everyone can feel comfortable sharing their ideas, concerns, and even their mistakes without fear of judgement. Acceptance of vulnerability creates a culture of openness and innovation. It's about creating a space where everyone's voice is heard and respected.

Recovery showed me the power of connection in the healing process. I can't stay sober alone. People often believe that the solution to addiction is just putting down your drug of choice. The truth is, the solution comes in our connection with others. Listening to others who think and feel the same way as you is incredibly powerful. My addiction brought me nothing but isolation, so it makes sense that my recovery is about the complete opposite. Think about it for a moment. How often do you think you're the only one who feels the way you do? We often believe that everyone else has got their shit together and we just need to pull up our big girl pants and get on with it. But all this does is breed shame. Shame for not knowing enough, or doing enough, or being enough. That shame keeps you small, trapped, silent. So, imagine a space where you can share exactly how you feel without the fear of being ridiculed or criticised. How might that help you? Your vulnerability can become the catalyst for meaningful connections, which can help to skyrocket your business to a new level.

Ultimately, it's about turning challenges into opportunities for growth, understanding that resilience is not the absence of vulnerability but the strength to rise again. Setbacks are part of the journey. Vulnerability has the power to inspire. Being open about challenges and triumphs creates a narrative that resonates with others, inspiring them to embrace their authentic selves.

Just like recovery taught me to embrace my weaknesses, I've taken that lesson into my business world. It's not just about personal growth — it's a daily part of how I run things. Success, I've learnt, isn't about acting like I've got it all together. It's about seeing the beauty in imperfection and letting vulnerability be my strength.

Embracing Setbacks as Spiritual Lessons: A Transformative Approach in Business

Just like my weaknesses, setbacks aren't stop signs; they're lessons guiding me to a deeper understanding of this business adventure.

In the usual business script, setbacks are seen as roadblocks. But in my book, they're more like stepping stones. They're chances to grow, learn, and understand the entrepreneurial journey a bit better.

Recovery gave me a tough spirit — one that didn't break when things got tough, but got even stronger. I always knew I would face challenges; the fear of relapse is extremely real. The worst thing is that it always gets you when you least expect it. A walk on a sunny day, after a 12-step meeting, listening to a particular song on the radio, has all made me want to reach for the wine. But I have always been prepared for them. They may catch me unawares, but each roadblock has become a stepping stone for me to do the right thing, learn how strong I am, and bringing that spirit into my business means knowing that setbacks don't mean failure. They're chances for my spirit to flex. Proving strength isn't in avoiding challenges but in dealing with them like a boss.

Every setback is like a classroom where I get a crash course in life and business. It's a chance to dig into what went wrong, rethink my plans, and roll with the punches. I have failed more times in business than I have succeeded, and at first that was a bitter pill to swallow, but this learning, like the lightbulb moments in recovery, is a big deal — it pushes both me and my business to grow.

Setbacks in business are humbling experiences, reminding me I don't know everything. Staying down-to-earth means being open to the lesson's setbacks bring, knowing every challenge is a chance to fine-tune my game. It's about taking an inventory and asking myself questions; What did I do well? What could I have done better? What will I do differently next time? All the failures in business have taught me something and can bring hidden treasures. They might steer my business in a new direction, leading to surprises like unexpected opportunities, cool collaborations, or bright ideas. Like my nutrition coaching business. I started that at the beginning of 2021, but less than a year later, it had gone nowhere. I had some success, but my heart wasn't in it. But if I hadn't had started that business, it would have never led me to the business I have today. It had to happen that way. So, when you look at it like that, did I even fail?

It's about seeing past the problem and spotting the good stuff hidden in the setback. They lay the groundwork for a sturdier business. It's about setting up a business that can handle the ups and downs, roll with the punches, and come back stronger after every failed attempt.

Basically, setbacks are the bricks that build a business that can handle anything. Recovery taught me to go with the flow, and that's a vibe I've brought into my business world. Setbacks aren't just about personal growth — they're chances to build a team that's ready for anything. A business that learns and adapts from setbacks is a business that can handle whatever comes its way.

Setbacks, viewed through the lens of lessons, aren't roadblocks but opportunities for growth, and my daily spiritual practices serve as the compass that guides me through the transformative journey, turning each setback into a stepping stone of resilience and wisdom.

Daily Spiritual Practices: The Secret Sauce to Business Brilliance

Now, let's dive into a game-changer: my daily spiritual practices. These aren't just rituals; they're like the magic potion that brings a touch of wizardry to my business journey. And here's the best bit–they aren't some abstract concepts but real-life tools that I've honed through my recovery and brought into my entrepreneurial adventure.

Meditation as a Mental Reset

Imagine a cluttered desk. Meditation is like clearing away the mess, creating a clean slate for fresh ideas and focused thinking. In the chaos of normal everyday life, let alone business, meditation has been my mental reset button. I admit, it took me a long time to understand meditation. How on earth was I meant to stop thinking? But after years of practice, and yes, this does take practice, I realised it's not about zoning out; it's about dialling in, getting in tune with my inner self, and letting go of the noise that hinders clear decision-making. Social media, other people's opinions, even our own inner critic, all have something to say about how we *should* live our lives and what we *should* be doing with our businesses. Meditation drowns all of that out and just allows me to tap into the magic of me. It allows me to listen to the gentle whispers of my soul, follow my intuition, and make decisions that are aligned with the life I want to create for myself. It helps me cut through the noise and focus on what truly matters.

Journalling as a Business Diary

Journalling isn't just about scribbling thoughts; it's my business diary. It's where I record the wins, the setbacks, and the lessons learnt. It's how I process everything that goes on. My thoughts race. They flit from one to the other constantly, so journalling has become my saviour in slowing them down. In my head, the thoughts all combine to one huge mess, often leaving me exhausted, overwhelmed, and unable to make any kind of decision. Writing them down allows me to order them. It allows me to sort fact from fiction. It gives me insights into patterns, strategies that work, and areas that need a tweak, that I wouldn't be able to see if they weren't on paper.

Journalling is also how I connect with my higher self. It's about having a daily chat with the Amy I want to become. It might sound woo-woo, but it's my anchor. Connecting with my higher self is like having a wise business partner–someone who provides clarity when things get fuzzy, resilience when the going gets tough, and a steady focus on the path ahead. Where mediation helps me to create an awareness of my thoughts, journalling is the tool that helps me take those thoughts in a new direction.

Gratitude as Business Fuel

Gratitude isn't just a warm and fuzzy feeling; it's fuel for my business engine. Taking a moment each day to appreciate the wins, big or small, creates a positive vibe. Whether I write them down, or follow a guided mediation, both morning and night, I take just a few minutes to really tap into what I am grateful for. It's like filling up the tank with good energy, which reflects in my approach to challenges, collaborations, and the overall atmosphere of my business. It motivates me to keep on going, because believe me, there are often times I want to give up. It's just too hard some days, but then I remind myself of who I am. I survived rock bottom so I can survive a rough moment. I remember that it actually isn't about me. It's about the hundreds of women I help in one way or another, every single day, which is why they are always on my gratitude list. They help me far more than they will ever know, and I can't thank them enough for that. The good and the bad, I am grateful for it all because it all had to happen to lead me to this very moment.

As I put these words on paper, I feel the weight of my story. It's not some groundbreaking tale; many entrepreneurs have turned their lives around after quitting drugs and alcohol. But here's the beautiful part — we are all unique, including you, and that's pretty fucking amazing.

Spirituality, like a wise friend, helped me grasp this. It reminds me that no-one else will ever walk my path exactly the way I do. Just think about it — you're the only person in the entire history of the world who can do what you do, your way. Consider this: You are an unparalleled force, a one-of-a-kind in a sea of billions. Your experiences, triumphs, and viewpoint are a special gift to the world.

In the world of spirituality and business, this understanding drives me forward. It's the spark that says, "Your journey, though shared in some ways, is uniquely yours." And the same goes for you.

As we wrap up this chapter, let's soak in the magic of our individuality. Let's celebrate the fact that, in this vast expanse we call the universe, we each have a solo — a melody that only we can play. Your story, your business, your journey — they are all notes in the grand composition of life, and each one adds a richness that only you can contribute.

So, here's to us. The spiritual warriors navigating our success with soul. May our journeys continue to weave their magic, creating ripples across the world. Let our journeys be a legacy of what wonders can be created when we embrace our true authentic selves, giving permission to women everywhere to know that there are no limits to what we can achieve.

Meet Amy

Meet Amy, the incredible life coach and storyteller behind the words above. She's not your typical entrepreneur – she's a survivor, a seeker, and a friend on a journey through sobriety and life. Amy's been through the trenches of addiction and discovered a unique path to resilience, spirituality, and creating a life you love.

After years as an active alcoholic, once going into recovery, Amy found that she had spent her whole doing the things that she believed would make her happy, only to constantly feel like there should be more to life.

Now, after spending almost 5 years working on her own personal growth, she lives her life her way, finding her joy, passion and purpose in helping others to do the same.

As a life and mindset coach, Amy brings a realness that hits home. She's not just sharing theories; she's dishing out practical wisdom from her own journey. Her words go beyond the norm, offering down-to-earth advice for those craving success and a deep sense of purpose in life.

Using a variety of cognitive behavioural therapy (CBT) techniques and *woo-woo* magic, Amy helps women to take control of their mindset so they can achieve their goals and love life again.

Amy is happily single, child-free and is often found on trips away across the UK. She has a passion for singing in her local Rock Choir, reading "who done it" books and binge-watching psychological thrillers.

LINKS

Facebook: https://facebook.com/amy.deards

Instagram: https://instagram.com/amydeardscoaching

Website: https://amydeardscoaching.com

Chapter Three

Charlotte Saunders

Exploring Spiritual Roots: From Childhood to Tai Chi

I had believed my first spiritual experience was when I bought my first crystal shortly after my eldest son was born. It was a beautiful snowflake obsidian heart shaped palmstone. However, on reflection, I realised that growing up in a Tudor farmhouse, I never truly felt alone. When I visited my paternal grandparents in their old cottage, I also never felt alone. I can't really describe the feeling other than a sense of warmth and almost being held - it was never scary but always reassuring and a feeling of love. However, in my maternal grandparents' modern build house I often felt alone and quite cold.

Whilst doing A' Levels, I started taking Tai Chi classes. This was the first genuine experience I had of feeling energy moving. It felt both odd but also reassuringly familiar. Over time, it has also become very clear that I have a strong sense of intuition, along with being clairsentient and clairvoyant. I can fairly frequently see those that have passed and can receive messages from them to pass on to people. This tends to be people within my circle who I have a close relationship or who I have an open-hearted connection with. However, I have also received messages for others with whom I don't have an immediate connection. I used to be able to see those who have died everywhere, but this became very overwhelming for me and so I asked for it to stop. One thing I have learnt is that you can ask Spirit to stop at any time and this will be done for you.

As my spirituality and soul connection have evolved, I have found people coming into my life who help me strengthen that connection and who lead me to other disciplines and areas of interest. These are also the people that are unafraid to ask me the hard questions. Questions that need to be asked to ensure that what I am doing is always coming from a place of soul and is for the highest good and is positive in all of its intentions.

Navigating Career Paths: From Psychology to Entrepreneurship

Outside of spirituality, I have lived a fairly normal life. I finished school and went to university and completed a first degree in psychology, and then completed a master's degree in forensic psychology.

I worked in prison for a short while and then worked for the police undertaking analysis of serious crimes for approximately 10 years. Forensic Psychology is something that people seem to be endlessly fascinated by. However, it is a tough and mentally demanding job and that is after you take in the fact that I was a young civilian female, apparently telling older alpha male officers how to do their job! In retrospect, it distanced me greatly from listening to my soul; I had to develop a very strong shutter to stop what I was seeing and reading from affecting me in my daily life and my relationships.

After I had my children, I worked in nurseries and then moved into working as a virtual assistant, eventually retraining as a bookkeeper. Now I work for myself doing bookkeeping and accounts for a variety of business types. However, my specific niche is working with spiritual and soul-led business owners.

One of the primary drivers for me to work for myself and from home was my children. Over the years, my middle child has had a lot of medical issues — at age 3, we noticed he was walking oddly and falling over a lot. After several appointments with a paediatrician, the doctor diagnosed him with hemiplegia (a form of cerebral palsy), and he then started experiencing a lot of stomach issues.

Finally, after numerous medical appointments, we learnt that the initial diagnosis was incorrect. He actually has a variant of Ehlers-Danlos Syndrome. The medical profession has since changed the diagnostic criteria for this and he falls into the gaps between the various types. They also noticed that he has a dilated aorta and is at high risk of an aortic aneurysm, so he undergoes annual reviews. Then, at age fourteen, they discovered he had an internal carotid artery aneurysm, which they check every two years. When he went off to university, he applied for his medical records and we discovered he had attended 825 medical appointments! So, as you can imagine, I frequently needed to be fully available for him. As a result of all of this, the whole family is under the 100,000 genomes programme in the hope that we can help chart the pattern of the condition and help those in the future.

In addition to this, my third child had also received diagnoses of autism, dyslexia, and dyscalculia. Because of this, and the general unkindness of teenage girls in groups, my daughter is now home schooled. The need for me to be available and to work from home continues.

It is really important to me to advocate for my children and to fight their corner and ensure that they have the best options available to them. Obviously, my involvement changes in terms of time needed etc as they age. For instance, my participation with my son at university is now limited to answering technical questions. I am still here for support and advice, but this is less intensive than the daily physio I had to be involved in before.

What also became clear during this journey was that I (as well as my daughter) had the same medical condition as my son. I do not have the issue with aneurysms but I *do* live with regular dislocations and subluxations plus a generalised level of pain. This means that I need to work around my pain levels and my energy levels. Interestingly enough, breathwork has become very much a part of my pain relief and my ability to manage my condition effectively.

Entrepreneurial Ventures: From Virtual Assistance to Spiritual Finance

I was very fortunate when an entrepreneurial friend who had established her own virtual assistant (VA) company took me on as a subcontractor. She needed support, and it was through doing this that we saw the need for bookkeepers who could actually talk to people and help them understand their finances and so I decided to train as a bookkeeper. I also knew that after working on my own and as my own boss for such a long time, I would really struggle to work as a subordinate to anyone else. I am not great with doing what I am told, so working for myself was the only real answer in the long run. Working with my friend taught me a lot about starting and running a successful small business. In fact, during lockdown, some friends and I started a 24-hour alcohol delivery service!

In addition, I am also a fully trained financial coach helping people to move past their limiting beliefs and see the abundance that can be theirs. I love working with these types of individuals and businesses. I not only share commonalities with them but also understand the challenges they face in recognising the value of their talents and charging accordingly. Understanding the true value of their work, many people struggle with undercharging; I can help them with this struggle through my financial coaching skills. On a more concrete level, I can help them by ensuring they are claiming all the applicable expenses, for example, the crystals that they use within their work, their tarot or oracle cards, these are all items which are legitimately used within their businesses and can therefore be claimed. I always get to know all my clients and uncover what is important to them; what lights them up and what their hopes and dreams are. By learning this about them, I can see what is important. This enables me to use my intuition to lean into the best way to achieve it and how I can help them get to that point.

By specialising and niching into this field, I have made sure that I have learnt all the intricacies of accounting for these businesses. Making sure that I can help them ensure that their business is serving them as best as it can, as well as enabling them to help others by utilising their universally gifted talents.

Embracing Spiritual Tools: Crystals, Pendulums, and Ho'oponopono

Crystals have been a part of my life for a long time and they are something that I use in my daily practices. I will intuitively pick a crystal to sit with and to have on my desk whilst talking with clients but also whilst doing my work and I believe that these crystals help me find the insight necessary to see the issues with my clients and their businesses and also help me find solutions and ways forward to assist my clients in their businesses. I have a qualification in crystal healing and whilst I have never utilised this modality in terms of the business, it is something that I use within my other modalities. While working with a client, I will often be moved to hold a crystal, and it will often become apparent why this crystal is being indicated to me. For example, when working with a client who has a blockage in their throat chakra, I may work with blue kyanite. In addition, I will often be moved to gift a crystal to an individual, as I know that this is something that will benefit them and which will help them move forward. My life with crystals and my relationships with crystals are a constantly growing and ever-changing thing which makes me excited to see where it takes me next.

I had a period a few years ago where I was constantly seeing Metatron's cube and that was something that I did not really understand at all at the time, but my investigation into Metatron and Metatron's cube led me to look into Angelic Reiki. I quickly realised that this was a modality that would be an important part of my life going forwards. I found a course running soon that was close to my home (the Universe in all its synchronicity showing that when you are on the right path, all the right things are laid out for you and within your reach).

I made some beautiful connections on this course and learnt the most beautiful modality - Angelic Reiki is a method whereby you use yourself as a portal for the angelic beings and Ascended Masters to heal the person you are working with, the healing and messages come directly from the angelic beings and Ascended Masters through me - at the same time you also receive messages yourself as the portal, you can also access past life information for both your client and yourself. It is a truly beautiful modality and one that I have used in my business. Metatron has had a tremendous influence on me individually and also on my business, and I like to communicate with Metatron regularly to tune in and listen to any messages and downloads.

Whilst training in Angelic Reiki, I came into contact with Saint Germain, who has since been a constant presence in my life. I have been told that he was in my timelines from a past life, and I certainly have a very close connection with him. He is the bright violet flame who passes me frequent words of encouragement, wisdom and is also very cheeky so injects fun as well - I never thought previously that communication with Angels and Ascended Masters would be a two-way conversation and that also it could be full of fun and laughter as well as the more serious and impactful necessary messages, for example after a week of St Germain not popping in, the next time he appeared he came with a chorus 'Look who's back, back again' which made me laugh and made me realise that spirituality does not always have to be super serious — it can also be light-hearted and joyful.

Tuning in and listening to messages from the higher self and from the divine realm are part of my daily practices that help me ensure that I am working from my own soul purpose.

Spirituality plays a huge role in my business, although it may not necessarily appear so outwardly. My preference is to work with other soul-led businesses, now this does not mean that the business owner is intentionally working from a spiritual place rather it means that the business owner is working from a place of passion and love for what they do — to me this equates to them working from their soul purpose. If they are working from a place of passion, then they are working within their zone of genius and are doing what the Universe wants them to do, which means they are already working in synchronicity with the Universe.

I have been using a pendulum and dowsing with it for years — frankly, I suspect I would be lost without my pendulum! Using my pendulum helps me to make decisions about which way to go and in which direction to move in general. Now, don't get me wrong. I don't follow this without thought. My questions are measured and purposeful and they are asked with planning and thought.

Using a pendulum is a really useful tool and is easy to use if you are already used to using your intuition. You will likely find yourself drawn to a pendulum. Always make sure that you spend some time with the pendulum you are drawn to before buying one. Have a play with it and feel the energy it contains. I always start by tuning in, ensuring I am grounded before asking the pendulum to show me yes and then to show me no (for me yes is generally up and down and no is clockwise circles but you will find your signs from your pendulum and you will learn the signs it likes to give to you), I then ask a simple question such as 'is my name Charlotte?' So that I can check that the pendulum and I are working in synchronicity, once I am happy with this I then ask the questions that I am seeking some clarification on. This is also a tool that I use with my clients and questions around their businesses. This, along with my intuition and clairsentience, means that I can help them see where they need to be and what they need to be doing to move forward.

Ho'oponopono is the Hawaiian art of forgiveness, which is often referred to as 'cleaning' as we clean the data shared between all of us which affects both ourselves and all of those with the shared data. By doing Ho'oponopono I hope to improve all of my clients' businesses as well as all those businesses and individuals that they interact with. It also means that this helps everyone who is affected by the shared data.

One of the main tenets of Ho'oponopono is that everything in the world is alive - the floor, our furniture, the seat we sit on, the roads we drive on, etc and so when we do the Ho'oponopono chant we are cleaning everything of all the shared data.

I recently had to fly home from a retreat at very short notice because of a family issue, I was on the last plane out of the airport before a large storm was coming in - once on the plane the pilot said 'we will do our best to get you there safely' not exactly what I had been hoping to hear! So at that point I decided the best plan would be to ask Archangel Michael to surround the plane with a golden bubble of protection and then I thanked the plane for what it was doing and for safely carrying us and I apologised within the Ho'oponopono for working the plane so hard, I then continued to do the Ho'oponopono all the way home - shortly before we came in to land the pilot came on and said that the flight was better than they had expected and that the winds had dropped so that we could land safely. Now, I'm not saying that definitely happened because of the Ho'oponopono, but I would be happy to acknowledge that the Ho'oponopono made a contribution to this outcome.

Harnessing the Power of Breath: From Breath work to Shamanism

At the time of writing, I have just graduated from my training as a breathwork practitioner specialising in Anna Parker-Naples' BreathHealing Release™ Method.

The breath is the very essence of who we are and through the distance we have put between ourselves and nature we have forgotten the importance and impact of breathing correctly and of utilising our breath as a tool with which we can alter of state of being, our state of consciousness and our well-being and health - in all areas, physically and mentally.

We come into being breathing and we stop breathing when our soul leaves our body to move to the next skinsuit so we cannot underestimate the importance of breath to every aspect of our being. The BreathHealing Release™ Method helps us to release all the physical, mental, emotional and somatic blockages and burdens that are holding us back from being fulfilled in our life in general as well as our spiritual life, the use of this method along with functional breathing exercises can make a huge difference.

Breathwork has changed my life in so many ways and has helped me to be able to further tune in to the whisperings of my soul so that I can fulfil my soul path. I am also nearing completion of my Shamanic training and a large part of this is also utilising the breath as a part of Shamanic Journeying. It is fascinating that when you look at so many of the ancient cultures and rituals and religions you see that all of them have breathwork within their rituals, often with music accompanying it (be it chanting or drums rhythmically being banged) before we separated ourselves from the earth we had such an appreciation of the importance of our breath and how this breath ties us in to nature. By changing the blood gas balances with our breath, we can access different brain wave states and this can help us process our emotions and to process trauma that is present within our body. Our body stores trauma that is not fully processed and dealt with and this can then cause us physical, emotional and psychological problems which can potentially wreak havoc with our lives. This trauma can be effectively processed and dealt with by the use of the *BreathHealing Release™ Method*. This method uses Conscious Connected breathwork to access altered states of consciousness and then uses various tools to access and resolve unresolved trauma and bring the person back to being free of this trauma, breathwork can be a truly life-changing modality for people.

Breathwork is such a fast and effective method of releasing and healing these past traumas and healing our relationship with ourselves that it is a shame it is so widely overlooked by the mainstream.

Training as a shaman feels like a genuine soul calling. There is something very ritualistic about the Shamanic way of doing things that calls to the very core of who I am and, potentially, who I have been in past lives. For instance, the Shamanic drumming calls us back to a less complicated time when we were much more at one with nature and living in synchronicity with nature - being less divorced from the real world because of our invasive relationship with technology, we have separated ourselves from the natural world and the rhythm and cycles of nature - we can get anything we want anytime we want so we are living in separation from the natural world that we are actually part of. Because of this, I encourage my soul-led clients to allow themselves to be nurturing and inward looking through the winter months so that they can blossom into spring with new ideas and products. Again as part of that we try to put things in place to ensure that there is enough cash flow to allow these entrepreneurs to follow this natural seasonal flow as I believe that by living in alignment with the natural seasons, rhythms, and cycles we are bringing ourselves into abundance as we are working with the natural world rather than being divorced from it or actively working against these rhythms that resonate throughout our very being.

The ritual of Shamanic Journeying is a core part of being a shaman. This ritual is where we connect into our Spirit Guides, Power Animals in the Lower, Middle, and Upper World, and where we are given information or something else to bring back with us. This can also mean bringing back information or totems for our clients and can involve soul retrieval or power animal retrieval. Shamanism is a powerful method of moving back to our roots and getting back in to the flow of the cyclical nature of the natural world, and also helping us to listen in to the wisdom of nature and of our elders and ancestors - those that came before us have many powerful stories to tell us that can help us remember our place in this cycle and help us to fully live as we are meant to, listening to these messages can help us live in alignment with both the natural world and our soul calling.

As a spiritual and soul-led entrepreneur, I aim to share all my messages, inspiration, and any relevant modalities with my clients. I have clients who are open to hearing that these messages are coming straight from Spirit, but several clients are not aware of this. This is a deliberate act on my part as I know that not everyone is open to hearing that these messages come from Spirit but that they are open to hearing these messages without necessarily knowing where they are coming from.

I am a firm believer that everyone is exactly where they are meant to be, and that they will hear what they need to hear when they need to hear it. There is no need for them to know the origin of the message, especially if this means that they will ignore it and refuse to listen to the information without a second thought. These messages from Spirit give me a deep insight that can help me decide how I can assist others. Being soul-led also means that I have the best interests of my clients at heart, which leads my actions rather than leaning into what will make the most money. As a clairsentient I can see where my clients can be and what they can achieve, and frequently I can see how they can get there.

I lead my clients to abundance through an honesty of purpose, whereby if we are all doing our jobs to the best of our abilities and with goodness in our souls, then abundance will surely follow. It is also central, as a spiritual and soul-led entrepreneur, to be mindful of profit and my values, there is a line of thought that has been popular in recent years that the more you charge the more people will want your offering, however, to me that grates and is not a reflection of the true value of something. I always ask myself if my pricing is in alignment with my values? Does it feel right at a soul level? Is the value of the potential transformation right? I also have to look at whether I am aligned with my clients and being prepared to say no to potential clients if they are not the right fit is something that I am more than prepared to do. It is so important to be in alignment with your clients in order to fully serve them and to ensure that the work you are doing is both beneficial and valuable to them.

Challenging Limiting Beliefs in Financial Coaching

As a financial coach, my coaching is much more about challenging and reducing the limiting beliefs we hold that keep us from achieving all that we could and keep us from the abundance that awaits us. For me, there are two parts to this which interlink — listening to the client, specifically to the actual words they are using when discussing certain topics and then questioning and challenging around these areas whilst also holding space for the client to reflect and look inwards, at the same time I use my intuition to feel where we need to go to next and what areas we need to address.

We do not learn logic until the age of seven, so everything we hear before this age we just accept without question and these become the stories that we repeatedly tell ourselves as we journey through our life. Therefore, the messages that we hear from our parents, our carers and those we are surrounded by can continue to affect our lives unless we start to challenge and question what we are telling ourselves.

For instance, if we were told that poor people are lazy, we are likely to assume that those who are on the poverty line are simply not working hard enough; if we are told that you have to work really really hard to earn money, then we will assume this means working *all* the hours available in order to have enough money. Clearly neither of these beliefs is completely true — there can always be occasions when either of these might be true but they are in fact the exception rather than the rule.

What they are doing is setting us up to believe that no matter how hard we work, we will never have enough money. So we become resentful of the work and of the hours we are putting in which leads us to feeling dissatisfied with life and can also lead to us feeling disenfranchised from the world generally as we see others growing wealthy from not seemingly putting in the long hours. In fact, what is important is that we have fulfilled our basic needs (i.e. food, water, shelter, and company). Anything after this can be considered as an additional or as a 'nice to have' rather than a basic need. When we view money and wealth through this lens, we begin to see that what we view as necessary (in terms of possessions) is often not a necessity but a luxury and that our 'need' for money is much less than we originally thought. In fact, at this point, it is often helpful to think of money as energy and then extend this idea to see our work as a form of energy exchange in return for pay.

When we view it in this way, it will become much clearer that what we are truly searching for in terms of our working life is an equivalent exchange of energy. The equivalency of our energy in the work that we are doing being equivalent to the energy of the money we are being paid. Remember that money is like oxygen — there is always enough to go round and that whenever the Bank of England fear there will be a shortage of money, they simply print some more. So if we treated money like we treated oxygen how much differently would we spend our lives and how much differently would we spend our money and what we would spend our time and money on would no doubt also be very different too.

The Shaman's Breath: A Holistic Approach to Business

The Shaman's Breath, whilst this may be initially seen to be a breathwork practice, it is important to note that breathwork is merely one part of it. It has multiple aspects and it will no doubt continue to evolve and change as the need arises and as time flows. It has been established to allow me to help spiritual and soul-led businesses to establish themselves and flourish as successful business, to help any of those businesses who are struggling and need help to either establish themselves or to regain lost ground particularly when they know in theory what they need to do but are struggling to implement these actions.

The Shaman's Breath was downloaded to me and is therefore bigger than me — it feels like something very special that will become a trusted helper within the breathwork space in particular and which will draw on crystal healing, Angelic Reiki, and energy healing in order to help as many people as possible move through trauma and move into being their true selves. I work with a numerology specialist who has helped me to ensure that everything for the business is as built for success as possible in terms of the Universe. Why? Because if our framework is organised for success, then this will drip through into our clients and their businesses and personal lives.

The Shaman's Breath is an amalgamation of all my different life experiences, lessons, and all of my modalities. It feels like things are coming together to make one amazing and transformative methodology. That is not to say that this will be a static methodology — I have no doubt that as I and others within the business grow and strengthen, more things will become part of the alchemical mix. It is so important, I believe, to be able to grow, change and evolve as things come into our lives and as we learn more and these are the teachings that we can integrate into our businesses and personal lives in order to become our true soul selves.

We (myself and my trusted helpers) will support these businesses to work in true alignment with their soul's purpose and their spiritual values so that they are in complete alignment and thus open to free flowing abundance in all avenues. In addition, we also work with those who have successful businesses but who feel that their business is not in line with their soul calling and/or is not in alignment with their spiritual values. The things that we reflect on with our clients are the things that are also important and relevant to us as a soul-led business: slow marketing that aims to connect with people with no 'buy now and get a bonus' no 'it's your last chance to get this before…' or 'don't miss out buy it before the price goes up' whilst this means that things may be slower to start it also means that our clients are invested in who we are and what are values truly are. I firmly believe that when we are in alignment and leaning in to what we should do, then success as a business will come with ease. This does not mean that astronomical wealth will just drop in your lap, what it means is that your vision of success will come to you — be that working 3 days a week or having spaciousness to enjoy a favourite activity.

I use all the modalities above to listen in and attune to my clients and to see what is out of alignment as well as what is in alignment. Sometimes it is so important to just stop and listen — to hear the silence and see what words are coming, to listen to the soul whisperings of the clients soul and see where their soul wants to go, what lessons they have learnt and what lessons they need to learn. It is only by listening to these soul whisperings that we can get a genuine sense of what magic is to come, and this can then inform us as to what steps need to occur so that we can help to facilitate the magic emerging. I have a team of amazing and trustworthy people who help me do this plus also several fantastic spiritual contacts who can help in specific specialised areas in order to help these businesses grow wings and fly.

The Shaman's Breath - Breathing Life into Your Business.

Meet Charlotte Saunders

Charlotte Saunders is a passionate advocate for integrating spirituality into entrepreneurship, with breathwork being one of the main modalities she uses. With a background in psychology and forensic psychology, Charlotte's journey into spiritual entrepreneurship began with her profound experiences in energy movement and intuitive communication. As a clairsentient and clairvoyant, she brings a unique perspective to her work, guiding soul-led businesses towards success with compassion and insight.

As the founder of *The Shaman's Breath*, Charlotte empowers spiritual and soul-led businesses to align with their soul's purpose and unlock their true potential. Through her financial coaching expertise, she helps clients overcome limiting beliefs and embrace abundance with authenticity.

Charlotte's approach to entrepreneurship is deeply rooted in her spiritual practices, including breathwork, crystal healing, Angelic Reiki, and the Hawaiian art of forgiveness, Ho'oponopono. Her commitment to soulful business practices extends beyond herself; she leads her clients on a transformative journey towards alignment, fulfilment, and prosperity.

With a compassionate heart and a visionary spirit, Charlotte is dedicated to helping others harness the power of spirituality to create thriving businesses that uplift both themselves and the world around them.

LINKS

Facebook: https://www.facebook.com/the.shaman.s.breath

Instagram: https://www.instagram.com/the_shamans_breath/

LinkedIn: https://www.linkedin.com/in/charlotte-saunders-cefc-micb-pmdip-4a91b0152/

Chapter Four

Joanne Lazarus

My name is Joanne Lazarus, and my journey through entrepreneurship has been one of self-discovery, resilience, and growth. Entrepreneurship has been my guiding force since childhood, helping me navigate through challenges as I grew up.

Unearthing Forgotten Memories: A Journey of Self-Discovery

I was driving to my simulated patient role in Liverpool, a job I do often as an actor. This entails performing as though I am ill for the medical profession and the Junior Doctor exams, but I'll explain more about that later. I like to use the driving time to discover myself, learn, and grow as a business owner. I was listening to a podcast because I did what all entrepreneurs love to do and use any spare moment to multi-task. And learn new skills.

There was a girl discussing trauma who resonated with me. Having a childhood of pleasurable memories, I had locked away moments of anything bad that had happened during my younger days. While driving on the motorway, this podcast sparked some forgotten memories in my mind.

Usually, I call myself the very confident person. Giving energies into my business life and equally within my social circles. At times, bringing the two together via network meetings to further myself as a business owner. I am always smiling and I always feel I can put some kind of negativity away into a box. Lock it up and address it at an appropriate moment.

I took advantage of the early morning drive from Manchester to Liverpool to listen to a podcast on my phone. I could absorb more crucial information to further myself along as the businesswoman I have proudly become.

This podcast was about trauma. The businesswoman I was listening to was giving her own traumatic experiences and how she overcame them to have the business she had today. I don't know why I felt drawn to this podcast episode, but listening to it made me realise the importance of moving forward in life as an entrepreneur. A spiritual pull within me drives me along. Not having any reason, I have this energetic power, this drive to Liverpool this day, answered a lot of my questions.

It unleashed two memories from the deep, dark recesses of my mind. I had forgotten about them, yet they were big, *big* memories of my life. Could these memories have be triggering me in some way throughout my life? To behave the way I do?

Since I have unlocked these memories, I feel I should put them down into writing because they are important. And they are a part of my persona. A building block, a part of me, making me the proud business entrepreneur I am today.

A Traumatic Christmas Eve

It was Christmas Eve. I must have been seventeen years of age. My dad had a shop in Bolton. It was called *Samson Sales*.

He was a business owner, a brilliant one who in those days had a family-owned shop. *Samson Sales* was a variety goods value retailer, similar to B&M, offering customers the high street brands at value prices. It transformed into a toy shop for Christmas. However, throughout the year, he sold shampoos, affordable tinned food, and cut price items that were accessible to the public.

Every weekend I would go into my dad's van with him to go to work with him. I would enter from the passenger side and he would drive. The van was green; it was a strange colour, lime-green, distinctive. In those days, shop owners would use a little leather wallet to store their day's takings and then deposit the money into what is called a night safe.

Christmas Eve was probably the busiest day of the year, as the public would come in buy last-minute gifts; presents, wrapping paper, gifts for their family.

Dad had dropped me off at a friend's house on the way home from the shop as I was having a sleepover that night. But the usual thing was I would grab his case from the passenger side of the van and take his case into the house. Which I did every Saturday. However, this time he dropped me off on route.

These were days before mobiles or text messages. We were still on land lines and dial up phones with connected ear pieces via curly cable. The phone at my friend's house rang. It was my mum — someone had attacked my dad.

What had happened? We had been followed home, that was what had happened!

As Dad got out of the van with his case in hand, three thugs attacked him with iron crowbars. One of them smashed across his stomach; the other smacked him in the head. They attempted to take his case, which my dad allowed them to take. However, the cash that they were after was not in the case.

Dad, being very security conscious, always used to hide the money. In this instance, the cash was in a brown paper bag, folded it up in his shirt pocket.

Not realising where his money was, the thugs never found the cash. However, my mum was inside the house. She heard a commotion outside and heard her name being screamed. It was my dad shouting her name whilst he was being attacked outside the pathway.

She ran to the door. By the time she'd opened it, he was standing on the doorstep with his head covered in blood. It almost looked like someone had thrown a bucket of blood over him *Carrie* style.

I wasn't there at the time of the attack, but that hasn't stopped my imagination picturing the horrific scene. It made me feel terrible. If I had been in the van with my dad, I would have been there. I could have saved him. I could have helped. In reality, if I had been there, it would have been more of a traumatic outcome.

The memory of seeing my dad in the hospital was within my vision and my mind for a long time. I saw him in that hospital. Lying there with cuts all over his face, speaking calmly to me. Maybe he was trying to be strong in front of me as I cried. It kept playing on my mind; only hours before, I had been sitting in the van with him. Being only seventeen at the time, my feelings were all over the place.

Dad had a friend called Norman. He was his mentor and best friend and always looked out for my dad. Although the case from that fateful day was recovered, it was empty. Would you believe Norman found it thrown into some scrub land? Dad ended up using that case as a table. He would rest it on his knees while sitting in his comfort chair, using it as a table as he ate his lunch or his dinner.

Fast forward eight years and I lost him to cancer. It wasn't long after that brutal attack, possibly only six months later, he started showing signs of illness. He went for various tests and the doctors diagnosed him with non-Hodgkin lymphoma. To lose my dad when he was only forty-nine was the most horrific, traumatic times of my life. I still have that very case to this day. I have it in a cupboard. Like the memory, it has been gently put away.

Did that senseless attack bring on Dad's cancer? They say stress brings about cancer lifestyle. When I think back about my dad's lifestyle, his diet wasn't great. He ate a lot of fast foods from the chip shops in Bolton where his shop was.

Loss and grief can shape your perspective of life negatively or positively. Now, I have my own children, but I am cautious as I navigate through life and running my own successful business. The reason I'm so vigilant has always intrigued me. Glancing around, I ensure I am not being followed. I make sure my bags are not visible in the car. It seems that the incident has haunted me ever since without me even realising.

A Father's Comfort in Times of Turmoil

Writing for this incredible book has opened up other memories I had long since forgotten.

A memory comes out of the darkness of having to stop in my car while driving through Salford. Having my bag taken from my car as I was stuck at the traffic lights. As I've already said, these were the days before mobile phones. I shakily drove to the nearest police station to report the incident, but the police officer on duty was not very kind to me. I remember it felt like I was a menace; as though I'd spoilt her break. I needed comfort and just wanted somebody to ask if I was okay? Yet there was nobody there for me. I drove home in fear; I felt lonely and couldn't comprehend what had happened. When I arrived home that night, I cried myself to sleep.

That night, I had the clearest vivid dream. He came out to visit me. It felt like I was transported back to a place of happiness. We were on a ship from a past holiday; I was back on that cruise, on that deck. Tears well up in my eyes as I write this, remembering when my dad hugged me on that dreamlike ship deck without saying a word. He was just there, wrapping his arms around me, as if to say, "I am here for you." That was the last time I ever saw him looking that healthy — in my dream.

From Childhood Entrepreneurship to Facing Adversity: A Journey of Resilience

I believe I have an inspiring journey. My story is a testament to the resilience of the human spirit and the power of self-belief. It's clear that my experiences, both the highs and the lows, have shaped me into the entrepreneur and person I am today.

My journey to become the entrepreneur began at a young age. I am taking you back again, to the same years where I was working in Dad's shop. This time, I want to show you the strength and determination.

The connection between my spiritual journey and present state of happiness is a beautiful aspect I am proud of. With an ability to find fulfilment beyond material success and to cultivate a positive, loving aura is a powerful achievement.

I was fortunate enough to have been working in a family retail business at sixteen. As a school leaver, working for a big company or going to university, just didn't seem to do it for me. I was happy living at home with my family. My first business was selling toys for Christmas as part of working in Dad's shop.

I would lovingly take toys from the stockroom of the shop and fill the lime-green coloured van. I had negotiated a deal with Dad that I would sell the toys, then pay him for the stock out of my takings. This allowed me entry into the world of business. My entrepreneur journey had begun.

The toy party revolution began my journey to sole entrepreneurship, even though I wasn't aware of it yet. Making extra money, over my usual weekly cash-in-hand wages from working in Dad's shop, was exciting.

I was a happy-go-lucky girl, not wanting for anything — life was good. I kept my little job going for a couple of years. At seventeen, I took on some of the responsibility of managing the family shop. This was alongside my Oriflame job, which I'll talk about later.

Life was to take a different path.

My world fell apart when Dad was diagnosed with cancer. For a while, at the beginning of his diagnosis, I kept his shop running. Thrown into the depths of keeping the business alive and hoping the staff would still be a good team. Together, we kept it ticking over until Dad's illness progressed and we had to sell the shop.

Once it sold, another dream life emerged. This one was to travel.

I put my energies into fulfilling my goal to travel. In my mid-twenties, I made my dream come true by working on cruise ships for five years, travelling the world and working in their retail operations.

Twists and turns of life took hold, and Dad stayed with us another eight years before passing away at the young age of 49.

Why am I sharing all this with you all this? How has my past influenced my present? What was my spiritual journey to make me who I am today? My past is part of my present. It is the foundation of the entrepreneur I am today. While I'm not a millionaire, I have a strong, spiritual, and loving presence that influences my thoughts and personality. The journey I have taken to reach my present position hasn't been an easy one. The spirit needs to give one strength and ability to pull through such times, to get through even the darkest of times.

After my father's death, the fun-loving life-lover disappeared for a while. Thankfully, while working as a sales rep for Trebor Bassett, I met and later married Raymond, who brought her back. Together, Ray and I brought three beautiful children into our world. As a family, we could beat anything. We had a dream of moving to Spain. It would be great for us and the children, so we did. I felt happy and complete. Sadly, the move to Spain soon turned from a dream into a nightmare. However, this challenging time lay the foundation for who I am today. But, I'll come to that later. I would like to share my entrepreneurial journey with you first.

Ventures in Direct Sales and World Exploration: Unravelling Entrepreneurial Spirit

When I was seventeen, I worked for a company called Oriflame. It was a skincare company, and I bought into the prospect of being a skincare consultant and hosting parties in people's homes.

I remember the day I joined Oriflame. At the time, all Oriflame consultants had little burgundy cases that contained all of our stock. I proudly brought my skin care range home. Looking at all the forms and paperwork that came with it filled me with joy. I soon got busy asking friends to have Oriflame parties for me. The importance I felt holding that burgundy case, I felt like an executive. I would imagine myself carrying my little case to board meetings. I was a real businesswoman for the first time in my life and I loved it!

However, the feelings of elation soon evaporated when my line manager started talking about growing a team. It was scary. She told me to go through my address book, ask all my friends if they wanted to be an Oriflame consultant too and be on my team. This was way out of my comfort zone.

I didn't stay long with Oriflame for long after that. However, the adventurous side of me was craving something more; I wanted to continue being an entrepreneur.

By the time I was in my mid-twenties, another lifestyle had firmly taken hold. I wanted to travel and see the world. The Universe rewarded me with a free ticket to see the world — working on cruise ships.

For five years, I worked in the tax & Duty-free shops for a passenger cruise liner company. I was back in retail, running the boutiques onboard various ships throughout the Caribbean and America. I loved having the responsibility of having my shop to look after, especially while travelling the world. My interest in culture, the world and how others love, led me to Europe, The Mediterranean, Norway across the Atlantic to Brazil, The Amazon, Mexico, and America.

I felt very privileged to be a part of the ship's staff and loved the lifestyle. I had everything I needed; a roof over my head, a job, and a varied environment. My cabin was my personal living space where I could retreat to if needed. The shop was just upstairs, only three decks up, so no long commute for me. The ship had multiple retailers, restaurants, swimming pool, etc. to keep me entertained during my down time. Add all this to the fact that I was travelling the world and having fun. It was the perfect mix for me to learn more skills and a base for where I am right now in life.

Having left the ships in my late twenties, I became a sales rep for Trebor Bassett. I was over the moon that the job came with a company car. It was my responsibility to visit all the shops listed on my route sheet. However, I did not have fixed working hours; as long as I visited the shops on my route sheet, I had the freedom to organise my day as I pleased.

Selling confectionery to local shops during my time at Trebor Bassett enabled me to win prizes and indulge in my passion for travel. I won trips to various places around the UK and an all expense trip to Cannes in the South of France.

Balancing Motherhood, Acting Dreams, and a Move to Spain

It was during my time with Trebor Bassett that I met and married Raymond and had our first child. Raymond was a successful accountant, so I left work and became a full-time, stay-at-home mum. The decision to give up work was easy. It was my time to take a break from my working life and raise our baby. During the evenings, I joined some acting classes; becoming an actor had also been a dream of mine.

The years went by and we had another baby girl. Being a full-time mum to our two children was something I loved. We had time as a family to go on holidays and have fun days out. I would always plan play dates, friends over for tea after school, along with trips to Wales and anything time and finances would allow. I thoroughly enjoyed my time with my two beautiful daughters.

As time went on, I started using my acting skills as a paid participant for murder mystery evenings being held in large local venues. I felt proud of myself that I was bringing money in. It wasn't much compared to Raymond's salary, but it was *my* money, and I had earned it.

When the girls grew up, we welcomed a baby brother into our family. When he was nine months old, my dream of living in Spain became a reality. Our move to Spain was exciting, a new phase for our family.

Only living the dream later became a nightmare that we needed strength to overcome. We suffered from bullying and financial difficulties. However, this only shows me the true strength of my spirit and my ability to overcome adversity. Through sheer determination to create a better life for me and my family.

Living as an expat for six years is already a big move and stressful in its own right. However, add opening a drama school into the mix, while raising our nine-month-old son and the layers of stress grow. The credit crunch of 2008 was also happening during this time. It was an exceptional period of my life that needed my positive approach, to save our family from a massive split. Living in Spain brought my entrepreneurial spirit out.

Triumph and Tribulations: From Dreaming of Drama to Battling Bullying in Spain

What was I going to do in a country where I could not speak the language? Being the determined cookie I am, I took myself off to lessons and threw myself into learning the language. I wanted to understand what was going on with other parents and the teachers at the children's school.

It was during the time in Spain, living in La Nucía, I had a dream to open my own drama school. I had the expat community at hand and wanted to give the younger members of the community an outlet where they could enjoy drama in their own language.

It was 2004 and a new social media platform was being launched — Facebook. I didn't understand what this *Facebook* was, so I set the wheels in motion and made posters for the local venues. It was posters and word-of-mouth that enabled me to begin my drama school.

I opened "*Drama Kidz*" with my vision and determination. We would offer drama classes, produce shows and pantomimes, and have fun evenings for adults. I remember it well; the business began on a Tuesday evening. The business prospered and later we launched "*Drama AdultZ*". Combining the two into shows that became prominent along the Costa Blanca. I became a producer and director, using those skills learnt when studying to be an actor.

We put on popular productions in La Nucía, which led me to organise an even bigger project. I took on a 500-seat theatre and set out to produce the show *Fame*. This catapulted my reputation as a drama teacher, which grew the popularity of *Drama Kidz* and *Drama AdultZ.*

However, as my business became more successful, the bad-mouthing started. Gradually, some local members of the expat community found it fit to ruin me. Facebook was a new tool, where those who needed to could use it as an open platform to use bullying tactics. I was soon a victim to a group of trolls, spreading the word that I was a fake actor and did not really know what I was doing.

My reputation amongst a few groups of people within the area where I lived became intolerable. I found myself the victim of a Facebook bully campaign because of the jealousy of another person who had a dancing school in the next town.

The camaraderie and friendships I had built through *Drama Kidz* were being corrupted. I believed people had to decide which drama school they wanted to attend. The whole thing was beyond my comprehension of anything I have ever experienced in my life.

The amount of controversy and bullying that went on broke me. It broke me more so than anything I had known in the past. Apart from the time I had lost my father.

We were going through some family financial problems because we had hit the credit crunch of 2008. Life was at an all-time low, money was non-existent, and we didn't know if we would lose our home. Do we buy food? Or do we pay the electric bill?

The dream life on the Costa Blanca had become the nightmare of all nightmares. Not only was I being emotionally bullied and a victim of ridicule, but we were close to losing our house and having to leave Spain.

With great heartache, we went back to the United Kingdom. Spain was not only breaking us, it was also breaking us up as a family. My marriage was failing. We had no money and my business was ending. The people who had bullied me had opened their own drama school, and some of my *Drama Kidz* students enrolled with them. In the end, I gave up the will to care any longer. So it was with great sadness we left.

Resilience Amidst Setbacks: Rebuilding in Manchester

I said *adios* to our life in Spain and the Costa Blanca. And along with my family, we came back to Manchester. By now, my entrepreneurial spirit had dwindled. My inner heart felt like it was in two and my energy had got up and gone. The strain of it all caused a split between me and my husband, so much so that sadly, we separated for a year.

What happened during our time in Spain totally cut my spirit into two. The jealousy of other expat business owners, the bullying, and the hate campaign. Plus, the banks recalling credit, putting our home at risk of repossession. However, looking back with hindsight, moving to another country taught me the value of a positive mindset and adaptability. Innate spirit, positivity, and hope became the key building blocks for survival. I can now embrace my genuine entrepreneurial spirit by exploring various business ventures, even if they are seen as failures by others. I feel I have a clear and deep understanding of the value of self-belief and persistence.

Back home in the UK is where the entrepreneurial journey really took a turn. Digging deep within my heart, I was back in Manchester, with no work, no house to live in, and a very unhappy husband. I was determined to get a "Nice Job". Thankfully, the latter came to fruition sooner than I had expected.

I remember driving past the football stadium during a shopping trip and thought; *I wonder what it is like to work at the biggest football club in the world?* A friend worked at the club and arranged an interview for me — they were looking for a tour guide. Football is a subject I knew

91

nothing about. However, as it was a top club in the football world, I envisioned myself working there. I was aiming high and knew this nice, little, part-time job would help me get there. I firmly believe that becoming a member of staff at Manchester United resulted from my job manifestation.

Luckily for me, the tour guide job was a flexitime (AKA flexitime) contract. A flexitime job allows employees to customise their working hours. This allowed me to earn money on my workdays and used my banked hours to fuel my forward vision. Having Manchester United on my CV gave me respect, but being a female with no football knowledge caused issues in a male working environment. However, I remained there for eight happy years and built up my knowledge, skills, and contacts, which I am immensely proud of myself for.

While I was working for Manchester United, I began various businesses. I became a wax melt queen, bath bomb seller, mascara expert, and an aloe vera ambassador, to name but a few, for MLM companies. However, my vision of becoming a successful business owner was slowly unravelling.

I loved my little wax melt business. It was growing, albeit slowly, so I moved production and storage out of my kitchen and into my garage. I did not know how to use Facebook or social media to grow my business audience, but it seems fate had other plans. I went into the garage one morning to start work and saw mice droppings all over my equipment and products. Yuk. I closed the business after that.

Next, I sold bath bombs. I bought beautiful handmade bath bombs from a woman running her own business from her home like I had done with my wax melts. She was making the handmade bath bombs and I would buy myself pretty baskets and bags and sell the bath bombs at craft fares. I loved it. It re-ignited my passion for being a soul-led entrepreneur.

It was during this time that I also landed a job as an actor, doing simulated patient work. Patient work simulation was completely new to me. In my first experience, I found myself in a sports centre in Sheffield that they had transformed into an examination room. The exam was for 100 doctors wanting to progress in their career as psychiatrists. My job was to act as though I had a mental illness or playing the daughter of somebody with mental illness during this exam. The entire experience was unique and like nothing I'd never known before. I still earn money as a simulated patient at various times throughout the year twelve years later.

However, I felt as though the people around me were ridiculing me. *Oh, you're so busy. You work at Manchester United. You do this simulated patient work. How are you fitting all of this in?* Remembering how I overcame the events in Spain kept the entrepreneurial fire burning and gave me the motivation to carry on.

My spirituality shields me from negativity. It would not let me listen to any negative thoughts my inner critic whispered or those well-meaning family members and friends sent my way. "*Oh what is she doing now*". My spirit nurtured the belief in myself; if I can get myself a job for the biggest football club in the football world, with no football knowledge, there was nothing I couldn't achieve.

However, there was a price to pay for "fitting everything in". I began to feel overwhelmed and stressed, which resulted in a mini-stroke.

The simulated patient work became more frequent – it brought in a higher income, too. So, in 2020, I decided it was time to leave my job as a tour guide for Manchester United. I loved I was earning money, yet not working every single day. The entrepreneurial spirit was flooding back into my life. It was making its way back into my heart, back into my passion. Ignited, and the spirit of wanting to be out there was returning to me.

Pivoting in the Pandemic: From Wedding Coordinator to Santa Claus

It was during 2019 that I started networking and joined a wedding group. I was spending a lot of my time helping people organise their weddings, without earning an income from it. That couldn't continue. Helping people was the best — it fired me up. I had to be more productive with my time and increase my income.

My organisational skills reared again. I realised I could organise weddings as an on the day coordinator. I formed my business and charged an appropriate fee for this service. To my utmost pleasure, I found myself in countless meetings with wedding couples within the various networking groups I belonged to. I was coordinating large weddings in venues, such as the Holiday Inn and the Piccadilly hotel in the centre of Manchester.

Then, imposter syndrome set in. How on earth could I pull that off? Who was I to coordinate weddings with 500 guests? Yet I did. It was a great success. I was getting clients and gaining a reputation for my newest venture.

Then there was a change of events. COVID-19 hit the wedding world. Large gatherings came to a stop, and overnight, my business had diminished. The football stadium also had to close. I was in shock, like most of the entrepreneurs in the world. What were my choices? Enjoy some downtime at home watching Netflix? No. I knew I had to channel my passion and spiritual energy into advancing my entrepreneurial journey.

It was November, and the run up to Christmas was about to begin. However, I had heard all the grottoes were closed. It was whilst sitting in my front garden, a friend drove by, upset and worried. He had no work on because he usually played Santa in various grottos around the area. I remember jumping to my feet and said in a happy, positive manner, if the kid can't go to the grottos, let's take Santa to them.

He looked confused but felt a sigh of relief when I offered to set up a Facebook group and an Instagram page; let's get some bookings! That conversation turned into a temporary seasonal business. Bringing in six grand! We were both Santa and Elf and brought lots of pleasure to the local families.

From Conversation to Calling: Embracing the Role of a Celebrant

January 2020 brought a rest for the body, but my entrepreneurial head was still whizzing. Large gatherings remained prohibited because of the UK's COVID restrictions. While walking in the park, getting my hour of fresh air, a friend mentioned that my acting skills would suit being a celebrant. This sparked something inside me and I started my search for a company who offered recognised training to become a celebrant. It is truly amazing how a business is born out of a conversation.

With the encouragement of other business owners, I stayed happy and fulfilled even when changing jobs. In 2021, I qualified as a celebrant and have a fulfilling business, helping couples to have the day of their dreams.

Writing this book has made me realise I put a great deal of effort into my businesses. I genuinely thought each one would give me the financial freedom and dream lifestyle I always wanted.

The skills I learnt while working in Dad's shop when I was younger have led to a life of travel and seeking adventure. I've met people from all over the world and enjoyed life whilst working and earning a living.

My entrepreneurial head still never stops, and surely, as I write the end of my given space in this book, I know there is more to tell. Another business idea is looming already, to complement the business I now have. A chance meeting to ignite my inner passion to live a full happy life of financial freedom and flexible working times, to also spend with the family. This is my inner spirit that lives on creating the passion that is within me.

Meet Joanne Lazarus

Joanne's entrepreneurial passion began at an early age. Realising, what happens in past experience, leads a way towards building blocks towards life as we know it.

For thirty years, work life has been acting based with an array of business and a discovery of a journey to lead her where Joanne is today.

With a love of travel, especially one for the high seas. Combining her knowledge of teaching drama and zest for seeking out new destinations,

She had the chance to teach drama to cruise ship passengers whilst on a part of a world cruise.

Having lived in Spain for six years, on the stunning Costa Blanca, Joanne opened her own drama school. Teaching drama and producing plays for the expat communities.

Returning to the UK and after many attempt at forming her own business, Joanne used her organising skills to open her own wedding event business "JL On the day", and became an on the day wedding coordinator.

Joanne quickly changed directions during Covid as used the time to retrain as a wedding celebrant, which is now her other business she has become to love.

Married to Ray a mum of three and loving her newer role in life as grandma to two cutie pies. Loves to eat Chinese food and met her idols Take That whilst out enjoying coffee in Starbucks, yes all three of them walked in. Joanne ended up having a cameo appearance on their 30th anniversary.

Chapter Five

Judith Rayner

Unearthing Wisdom: Embracing Adventure, Intuition, and Authenticity

Some of my best memories of childhood are those of going to Girl Guide camps with my mum. She was a guide leader and me, my older sister and brother, being too young to leave at home, went with her.

These were pretty much our holidays growing up and were in the days before health and safety went mad and made camping so much more restrictive.

I have brilliant memories of midnight (*probably more like 9 pm*) walks by torchlight through cow fields. Whole day 'treasure' hunts where the hunt was for our buried food, which we then had to try to cook (*having found buried matches and firelighters!*). Midnight feasts with lots of sweets on the last night, and generally being outside, a bit grubby, and often barefoot — the freedom was the best thing ever.

We foraged for firewood, built and cooked on proper fires, made things from wood, slept on the floor, told stories and sang songs round a huge campfire.

Those truly were some of the best days of my life – a little adventure and sense of freedom every day.

I remember desperately wanting fairies to be real. In my search for their homes, I would place little gifts outside and build miniature gardens for them. I spent countless hours exploring, playing, and using my imagination. I can still remember the joy I felt when my daughter believed in fairies and I happily joined her in making and leaving trinkets in tucked away places, for them to find.

The era I grew up in was parentally hands off – the latch key generation. Go out in the morning and, as long as you were back for tea, all was good. No contact, no phones – just fun, adventure, trust, and a telling off if you were late.

Funny that trust has also become a huge thing for me in how I run my business and how I deal with challenging times. Trusting that I have what I need and that there is plenty for everyone. Also, trusting those that are part of the challenge are doing their best with the resources they have right now, too.

Back to childhood freedom — there was a field, a wood, and a river behind my house. This is where I, my brother and his friends spent hours and hours. From building hay camps, swinging on a rope swing left by someone else, and fishing for minnows in the river. Getting up to mischief that no-one ever knew about. Again, a sense of freedom that has been an important value throughout my life.

Growing up and getting on with people.

As an eleven-year-old, I often found that I didn't fit in — I was quite serious. I possessed wisdom beyond my years and a firm sense of right and wrong, along with a heightened perception of what went unspoken. I could sense an undercurrent, notice a tiny look, hear a tone. Looking back, I realise I was pretty sensitive to what was going on around me.

With that being said, I wasn't a *sensitive* person in the way it's talked about these days. Throughout childhood, I often said the 'wrong thing', spoke out 'too much', and shared my wisdom, children called me boring and adults said that people didn't like 'know-it-all's. I learnt to not always share my wisdom or knowledge just in case someone thought I was being a boring know-it-all. But I learnt to be lighter. To be, and have more fun. Fun is definitely a value for me now, though it can take a while for people to see my kind of humour.

I was, and still am, fiercely loyal and couldn't understand others weren't. It hurt deeply, and I would withdraw and put up my barriers, which obviously made people more wary of me in return. I value honesty and trust and once betrayed I have trouble moving on — it hurts, and the trust must be re-built over a long time.

I like things to be right — to be honest and true. I resist following the crowd, though there's that younger part of me that wants to be part of the popular crowd. In fact, now I'll go the opposite direction, which can be detrimental to business — more on that later.

My mum took to Christianity in a big way when I was a teenager. I had not received a christening as a baby, and she wanted to rectify that.

However, because of my age, I would also have to be 'Confirmed — married to God'. It was time for me to rebel. Not in a big way, but with clever arguments and, eventually, out-and-out refusal to be 'confirmed'.

I found out later that her move towards religion was driven by the difficulties in her and my dad's marriage. My sister remembers huge arguments that I was blissfully unaware of, but something made me and my brother try our hardest to be funny and keep things light, picking up on the atmosphere and unspoken even then and trying to change it.

She stayed in the marriage for the 'sake of the children', determined that she had made her bed and was well and truly laid in it.

Although at some point we decided there was no way we were going to get married, if that's what it was like. Funnily enough, we have both gone on to be married. As of course, you learn that your parents' story isn't your own and you can create your own future.

At fourteen, as I was crossing the road outside school one day, a motorbike hit me. I ended up in traction at the local hospital with a broken leg for the entire summer. From my private room (it had a clear window), I saw lots of lights moving in the distance and wondered if I was witnessing UFOs.

We can rationalise this experience. I was still sedated. It could have been a combination of factors — who knows? However, that vivid memory has stuck with me all these years. I can't say for sure what it was or wasn't, but I'm sure that I was awake.

I had a ghost experience at my house one night — a girl sat on my bed — I couldn't move or speak, and it happened just the once. Again, was it a ghost or was it my imagination? Who knows?

I've always had a sense that there was something I was destined to do. Something that I was going to be really brilliant at and gain recognition. But at a young age I became fearful, and it stopped me from doing the bigger things in life for a long time. I can see now that this fear held me back, on and off, through the years into adulthood, too.

In my search for this special thing, I was waiting for a sign, or signs, to let me know. I tried many paths, enrolled in lots of different trainings, but never took them to completion or made 'successes' of them, before moving on to the next thing. My mum would have said, 'what are you doing now' or 'doing another new thing'. Now, I can see a pattern, a story forming. The fear of not getting it right or of failing the bigger, harder thing caused me to become distracted and attracted by brighter, shinier things.

But is it fear? Is it ADHD? Is it lack of self-belief or esteem or simply I hadn't found the 'thing' yet? Ignoring my intuition and inner voice and forcing things has always led me to make my worst decisions.

In my life, I've only experienced three long, serious relationships. My relationship history includes a three-year one at 18, another from 23 to 30, and my current one started when I was 31.

During the first ten years with my now husband, our focus was on working and earning money. We were living our best lives; travelling, living in a *nice* house, having *nice* cars, and doing whatever we wanted. We had few ties and were rarely at home — even our neighbours would say how they never saw us. Our travels took us to far-flung places such as Thailand, Jamaica, Australia, and America. We enjoyed lovely weeks on Greek Islands, and other European destinations.

I fell in love with huge open spaces after our long mountain walks in the Lake District, Dales, and Fells here in the UK. The awe of being up high, surrounded by vistas and big skies. Walking boots became a symbol of freedom for me. You could walk on or through anything and keep warm and dry! Proving true that old adage *'no such thing as bad weather, just bad clothing'*.

I've been on one long self-learning journey of discovery for the last twenty years — pretty much since deciding to have a child. Before that, I was too busy with work and relationships to reflect on my true self or desires. Or if I did, I soon pushed aside or diluted my thoughts based on what my partner wanted. I was quite influenced by what others thought of me instead of trusting myself.

My one and only child, a daughter, turned out to be my biggest teacher. A very spiritual lady once told me that Charlie was sent to teach me. That my daughter was wise (*just like I was as a child*), and my job was to listen and grow however hard the lessons. Honestly, at times, they have been the hardest lessons of my life. However, I have definitely become more attuned and stronger with age.

The Start of My Entrepreneurial Journey and Being a Lifelong Learner of Stuff!

It wasn't a success story, a fast track to money story or a straight road story.

I wasn't a big shot in the city who burned out and had an epiphany. I wasn't wealthy, working too hard, but unhappy in my soul. A huge life event or tragedy did not change my life.

I was a normal working woman who was doing quite well. I worked my way up to middle management and happily stayed there for many years, managing teams and developing my staff. All the time adding to my skills, taking every training offered — train the trainer, staff assessment, mentoring, management and leadership, coaching and generally honing my people skills on the job. I also had the opportunity to join extensive projects that allowed me to travel, working with teams and managers in Europe.

What I didn't realise was how all of this would lead me to having my coaching business. All the time, I was also honing that early sense of intuition that I now tap into for decisions and when working with clients.

While continuing to work full-time, I trained and subsequently qualified as a life coach. Helping people positively change their lives, whether personal growth or finding balance. After stumbling upon my tribe (more on that later), I transitioned into Business Coaching. I found combining the life elements with ambition and aspiration to be satisfying — I could really make an impact. After being made redundant, I learnt about NLP. NLP helps make positive and lasting changes by understanding patterns in language and behaviour. Eventually deciding to bite the bullet and start out (cluelessly) on my own with my first coaching business called 'Powerful You'. I still own the domain name and might one day resurrect it as my work with women shifts again.

Starting and staying in business has been a real growth journey on all levels. It has been messy, confusing, costly, exciting, lonely, stop/start, frustrating, inspiring, and much more. I'll share my wiggly, wonky journey, and the pillars that have kept me grounded along the way. I'm a late starter and even later to find what I now believe is what I'm here to do.

These things don't always happen through a decision. They come about through listening to the messages, following the tangled threads and trusting that you can change, start or renew at any time.

Some of us never have that epiphany, huge life story or massive *why* that we're told we need to be successful.

Some of us come about things because we can't imagine ourselves doing anything else once we've got an inkling or stumbled across the 'thing'.

In my case, it was a definite stumbling across that got me start. I was training to become a counsellor, had done stage one and two, and was getting ready to move onto the certification course. Because I had a full-time job, I had to ask for flexible hours in order to attend college for half a day each week. This was before flexible scheduling was popular in workplaces — they refused my request.

Now what? I couldn't do the course I'd already been working towards for a year.

A friend of a friend was training to be a life coach and was asking around for willing volunteers to practise on. I'd never heard of life coaching but said yes, as it sounded interesting. After just one session, I was hooked.

Counselling — what counselling!? This was way more powerful and positive than going over and over the pain and problem again and again, staying stuck. Yes, a life coach acknowledges an issue, but then it was about how to move forward and create change. It was amazing and brilliant, and I could see just how powerful being a life coach was.

I had found my *THING*!

But my business journey has not been a straightforward, linear path to success. Instead, it resembled more of a wiggly, wonky road, full of unexpected twists and turns and plenty of mistakes, too. But I can see the learning in all of it now, and in those twists and turns lay the seeds of my growth and resilience.

Fairly early on, I fell out of love with coaching — well, not coaching itself, but the coaching industry, which I felt was toxic.

The coaching 'gurus' of the time were pushing really questionable and manipulative sales/success techniques. Tapping into peoples' pain, making crazy promises, having very loud and forceful sales pages. These tactics just didn't sit well with me. In the end, I threw my toys out of the pram and decided if this is what you have to do to be successful in this online coaching industry, then I don't want to be part of it.

Exit stage left — Judith has left the building.

It wasn't until being made redundant some years later that the whole coaching thing crept back under my skin. My daughter was two and a half years old and I was 43 (*told you I was a late starter*).

I used part of my redundancy package to retrain. Having been interested in NLP for a while, I signed up for a taster weekend at The London School of NLP.

That light bulb moment of recognition struck again. The power of language, working and banishing limiting beliefs, altering our view on the world and how we interact with it — WOW!

As I continued to learn and then qualified as an NLP Practitioner, I also fell back in love with coaching.

Thankfully, things had begun to change out there. Some people, namely women, were doing business in a more ethical, heart-led way and I could see how it might just be possible for me, too.

Each time I've changed direction slightly, stopped or started, I have known deep down that something is or isn't right — intuition.

Networking

My first ever networking meeting. A room of some forty women who were all doing things, and creating things. Collaborating while still juggling life and children, all in the name of contribution and the freedom to work around family.

Blown away — I had found my tribe — the people I wanted to work with, get to know, and help as a coach. A few became great friends. I'm still connected to many of those in the room that day, via social media (*love or hate it, the power to stay connected is like nothing else*).

Connection is another tremendous value of mine. So, all the business groups, masterminds, coaching packages, etc. that I've run have been for small groups or one-on-one. I love to really get to know people and their challenges. This gives me the knowledge so I can offer really personalised thoughts, questions, and feedback. I can get under the skin of their business and how it fits them and their life. In fact, most of my current podcast guests, I originally met through networking going back as far as 15 years ago.

So not for me the huge memberships and cookie cutter programmes selling to the masses. No signature programme that, for me, felt restrictive. Simply personalised, intuitive coaching is my path. I literally get goose bumps when I know we're onto something or have stumbled across a nugget of gold yet undiscovered.

Walk and Talk Epiphany

For what felt like 'forever' I felt I had chained myself to the laptop, stuck at my desk, on my own, trying to get my business online and was getting very close to throwing the laptop out the window. I was lonely, frustrated and full of doubt (*again*) about whether I could do this. I was learning stuff I had little interest or skills in but thought I 'should' be doing.

One day, I was listening to something different, a more spiritual leaning, and the trainer said something like '*do what you're good at in a way you love*'! Really? I thought. You can do that? My hand grabbed a pen and 'walk and talk' and 'walk and talk 4 success' were on the page before I could consciously form the words. No thoughts, no plan, just those words arriving on the sheet in front of me.

I felt ridiculously excited, could feel it in my body, and yes; I danced a little jig.

The idea was born, and eight years later is running still. Other women were tired of being isolated, the online push, the lack of connection, and also desired something different.

Taking my coaching out on foot helped me discover the deep impact that being in and working with nature provided. It added to my learning with Nature as Co-facilitator in the coaching process. I could work within nature to help my clients transform and heal.

But perhaps the most profound evolution in my journey has been more recently. I realised I wanted to take things deeper with my clients — beyond conventional coaching methods. So, with my perceptive radar switched on, I gently sent out the feelers in search of what my intuition was looking for.

After a couple of years, I discovered breathwork. Breathwork is a holistic way to heal and learn about oneself through conscious breathing. As a breathwork coach, I embrace the power of the breath as a catalyst for personal transformation, guiding others on their journey toward optimum health, mental well-being and self-empowerment, which is perfect for business.

What else have I done? You'll see from my bio that I was a radio podcast host — 'Rebel Entrepreneur'. Now, what do I mean by that? I'm not a massive disruptor. Yes, I was one of the first to take coaching out on foot into nature, but I'm not a 'thought-leader' or a loud 'out there' person.

The rebel in me refuses to follow the crowd to 'make money' — to do what others said I should do — remember I tried that! If there's a buzzword or style, I'd push the other way, sometimes perhaps to the detriment of my business and bank balance.

I see myself as someone who loves to learn and is always curious. However, I can easily get distracted and I'm always drawn to new and exciting things. As such, I have spent thousands of pounds, hundreds of hours and a huge amount of energy seeking, training and studying. I've enrolled in various courses and programmes over the years; covering topics such as productivity, podcasting, marketing, and copywriting. My fifteen years in business has been one long learning and growth journey. If I had focused on one thing and hired help, maybe I would have earned more. But for me it's less about the money and more about my development, joy in what I do and, of course, FREEDOM.

Looking back, I can see the mistakes. I would do a few things differently, but I can see and appreciate everything that this wonky path has given and taught me. I bring all of my lessons and experiences into the mix when helping my clients achieve what they want to achieve in a way they love, too.

The Destination

I don't think we ever truly arrive at our destination in business — there isn't a fixed point that answered everything. Even if we think we have reached a turnover figure or a milestone that is 'IT', the chances are that the journey will have changed us and altered the destination. Take any of the big names, like Apple, for instance. They never stop. Their mission is so big that the game can never be over.

As a small business, accepting the journey as 'the thing' rather than the destination makes everything more enjoyable and energising. Any mistakes or wiggles in the road are simply part of the adventure — an opportunity to see it for what it is, a step in a long journey.

Finding breathwork, I feel closer to the destination of what I'm here to do than ever. But it's not breathwork itself, rather what I can do with it — the impact I can create through helping others. I know that focus will change over time — the who, what, how and when. I'm open to possibility and trust in what it can bring and where it will take me.

Since those early days of networking and finding my tribe, I've mostly worked with women. Women are incredible, strong, and powerful, while also tenacious and creative. I'm always inspired by and learn lessons from those I work with. My networking days opened my eyes to the fact that all was not what it seemed. The networking face — lippy applied, beaming smile, and talking confidently about business — often hid a soft underbelly. A façade hiding worry, loneliness, doubt and overwhelm. Add in juggling life, supporting struggling teens or older parents, and growing your business, the emotional load is immense for these women.

Today, it's these women I support. Women who have businesses and are the caregivers to teenagers or older parents. They feel like there's no space left for them, and that their business is suffering because of it. They are full of anxiety, guilt, and possibly even shame. Finding calm — the space and strength to keep going seems like a dream and seeking distraction by watching Netflix, seems like a good idea.

But I promise there is an AND between the struggle and juggle — an AND where self-compassion, kindness, and resilience lies. We can remind ourselves of our incredible pool of resources. By taking a step back and taking a breath, we can reconnect to ourselves and what truly matters. We can change our view on the world, which, I assure you, creates a ripple effect with those around us, too.

When I was going through some pretty dark days in recent years, because of a child with mental health issues, walking in nature was my solace. Alone with my thoughts but calmed by the sounds, scents, and scenery, I could be present and tap into my knowing and inner guidance. We all know that 'putting on our own oxygen mask first' is the way to help others, but so often, we don't do it.

Walking, nature and breathwork are your oxygen mask.

I help by taking women out and away from where the issue is — usually the home. My programme combines walking, nature, NLP coaching, and breathwork to help you explore and deal with hidden emotions and thoughts. We release and let them go. I share tools and strategies, and my clients rebuild a belief that things can be different. Things can change. There is a huge amount of trust needed — trust in self, trust in the person struggling and trust that there is an AND between everything to find oneself again. And a trust that we can do hard things and have a business.

The Future of My Business

I will continue supporting women like me. Those women going through or coming out of traumatic experiences, especially those because of looking after a struggling teen. Offering support while they find the space and the AND. Releasing trauma and guilt along the way and 'after'.

Do you feel as though you are hanging on by your fingernails? Shoulders up by your ears? Catastrophizing the now and the future? On high alert for the slightest thing? Living with constant anxiety and adrenaline coursing through your body?

As I conclude my chapter in this book, I hope you have experienced resonance and reflection, seeing your own journey in the stories I've shared. Now, I invite you to consider this not just as an ending, but as an invitation to a deeper, more personal exploration of what lies ahead.

Maybe you've encountered a similar sense of direction in your own uncertainties, as I have in my childhood escapades and entrepreneurial hurdles. Trust is crucial — trust in yourself, others, and the journey. Like you, I have travelled this path without perfect foresight, but with a faith in the lessons each experience offers.

If you feel overwhelmed by the demands of life, I offer a range of tailored services designed to meet you where you are. Whether that's juggling family, business, or personal well-being. You can choose from immersive retreats, small group programmes, or personalised coaching sessions.

Services Overview:

☐ **Retreats:** Dive into immersive experiences where you can find peace and clarity, surrounded by natural beauty. These retreats offer space for reflection and renewal.

☐ **Group Programmes:** Become part of a close-knit group that offers support and guidance through shared experiences. Using coaching and transformative techniques such as breathwork.

☐ **One-on-One Coaching:** Private sessions that address your individual challenges and help you move past limiting beliefs.

Embrace the chance to rediscover who you truly are and begin a life-changing journey of self-discovery. Take the next step and book a complimentary consultation to explore how we can collaborate in pursuit of your dreams and a fulfilling life.

I am here to support and guide you as you explore the depths of your own inner wisdom. Together, we can uncover your hidden strengths and empower you to lead a more fulfilling life. Thank you for sharing this journey with me, and I look forward to our paths crossing in the chapters to come.

Meet Judith Rayner

Judith Rayner, also known as *The Business Walker*, is a bit of a rebel entrepreneur!

After trying to fit herself into pre-prescribed 'success boxes' and almost throwing everything out of the window (*including the laptop*)

Judith knew she wanted to do things differently in her coaching business and put the idea of a *Walking Business Mastermind* out to her network. The fact it's still going nine years later, says it all. She wasn't the only one wanting connection to others, to nature, time away from the desk and support from like-minded women.

Judith found opportunities to follow her passions of walking and working with business women. Even through the pandemic lockdowns and restrictions of 2020-21, she took *Walk&Talk* online, and hosted remote sessions.

Judith has over 15 years of experience in coaching, mentoring and NLP. She uses a combination of modalities, including deep transformation breathwork, to help women who have businesses and are dealing with difficult situations like troubled teens or elderly parent care. Judith combines coaching, walking, and breathwork to support her clients in finding clarity and creating space.

Judith lives in beautiful Sussex in the UK with her husband, child, and crazy cat Rosie and can walk straight from her front door into the countryside. Travelling a little further for big hills, skies, forests, or the south coast when the mood takes her. When she's not walking, you'll find her reading, dancing or doing some kind of learning — a perpetual student of life!

LINKS

Facebook: https://www.facebook.com/walkandtalk4success

Instagram:https://www.instagram.com/judithrayner_thebusinesswalker/

Website: https://www.walkandtalk4success.com/

Chapter Six

Kim Brockway

Soulful Success: Navigating the Path of Spiritual Entrepreneurship

Welcome to my chapter in *Spiritual Entrepreneurship: Navigating Success with Soul.* I am deeply grateful that you have chosen this book. It's a true passion project reflecting my lifelong journey, intertwining spirituality and entrepreneurship. From an early age, the profound connections between body, mind, and spirit captivated me. I was always questioning beyond the apparent and exploring what lies beneath the surface of conventional wisdom.

This chapter unfolds the story of my entrepreneurial evolution. From founding Brockway Gatehouse in 2019, a sanctuary for authors to refine their narratives, to the inception of Wessex Wise Woman in 2024. This new venture marks a pinnacle in my journey — where ancient wisdom and modern spirituality converge. I'm offering a haven for those seeking self-discovery, healing, and empowerment.

Brockway Gatehouse was the seed from which my spiritual enterprise grew; a place where creativity and spirituality met and flourished. Here, I learnt the delicate art of balancing professional guidance with personal growth. I was helping authors to not only polish their manuscripts but also explore their inner landscapes. Through my work as an editor and coach, I discovered how spiritual practices can positively change businesses. This inspired me to adopt and promote these principles.

In 2024, inspired by a deeper calling, Wessex Wise Woman was born. Within Brockway Gatehouse, it shows my expertise in business and my strong ties to pagan traditions and earth-centred spirituality. The principles of my editing business and spiritual practices merge to create a distinct space centred on craft, creativity, and meaningful connections.

While reading this chapter, I encourage you to discover how Wessex Wise Woman has transformed my business approach and provided clarity on my path to success. Discover the transformative power and deep fulfilment that emerges from blending spirituality and business.

This chapter is more than a narrative; it reflects my dedication to living authentically and guiding others to do the same. Read my personal stories, practical insights, and how I integrate spirituality in business. I aim to inspire and empower you — whether you are just beginning your path or are well on your journey. Let's embark on a spiritual entrepreneurship journey, embracing challenges and triumphs.

May the wisdom shared here ignite your spirit, bolster your courage, and strengthen your resolve to pursue success with soul.

The Pagan Path Unveiled

In the medieval city of Salisbury, just a short distance from the mystical Stonehenge, I've always felt a strong bond with ancient paganism. The connection I had influenced who I am personally and professionally, but it often caused conflicts in my earlier careers. In my roles at a local high street bank and as a teaching assistant in Church of England (CE) primary schools, I found it necessary to hide my spiritual identity. This involved keeping my silver pentagram necklace hidden beneath my clothing to prevent any conflicts.

However, embracing entrepreneurship as a fiction editor and coach marked a turning point. It allowed me to incorporate my pagan beliefs openly into my business, using tarot cards, crystals, and Moon phase rituals. It took time for this shift to occur. As I became more confident in using these techniques, they not only enhanced creativity but also allowed me and my clients to express ourselves genuinely.

The Turning Point: Leslie Thomas and the Money Confidence Coaching Connection

Meeting Leslie Thomas, a money confidence coach, during our time on the parent teacher association (PTA), altered the course of my journey. Leslie showed me how to overcome financial challenges and personal obstacles using visualisations and path-working techniques. Her NLP-based approach, coupled with her deep understanding of the subconscious, inspired me to incorporate these methods into my coaching more formally. This combination of skills helped me in clarifying my objectives and honing in on the specific group of people I wanted to help and how to do so.

Podcasts, Path-Working, and Personal Development: The Anna Parker-Naples Influence

Thanks to Leslie, I discovered Anna Parker-Naples and her podcast, *Entrepreneurs Get Visible*. This podcast became a major source of inspiration for me. Anna's firm belief in maintaining authenticity and ethical standards in business mirrored my core values. She also emphasised the importance of personal development and self-care. Anna's challenge and retreat showed me how to blend spirituality with business strategies effortlessly. She used meditations and hypnosis in the 5-day challenge and used oracle cards on her day-long retreat.

The retreat, an intimate gathering at Anna's family home in Oxfordshire, was transformative. Engaging in meditations, journalling, and hot seat business sessions under the glow of a full moon. I experienced firsthand the powerful blend of community support and individual introspection. This experience not only enriched me spiritually, but also had a profound impact on my professional path. It helped me to crystallise the concepts that would shape this very book.

Embracing My True Self in Business

Today, I no longer hide my pentagram necklace. Instead, I wear it as a badge of honour — an emblem of my journey towards integrating my spiritual and professional identities. Through their efforts to promote diverse spiritual practices, the Pagan Federation has empowered individuals, including me, to live and work authentically.

These narratives from my life chart the course of my professional evolution. However, I hope they also showcase the potential for personal beliefs to enrich and guide successful business practices. Join me in discovering how your personal beliefs can guide your professional journey. Let's delve into the fusion of spirituality and entrepreneurship.

Breathing New Life into Coaching

Anna Parker-Naples, with her wealth of experience as a master practitioner in various methodologies, introduced a transformative opportunity: The Influential Breathwork™ Coach certification training programme. This was an opportunity I couldn't pass up, knowing the impact it could have on my own practices and the potential benefits for my clients.

Breathwork has become a cornerstone of my coaching. Especially when dealing with new authors overwhelmed by anxiety, imposter syndrome, and the stresses of creative life. Initially, I used my path-working skills to help them visualise their success. But integrating Anna's BreathHealing Release™ method of breathwork has allowed me to take my support to the next level. Thie BreathHealing Release ™ method enables profound changes at a subconscious level. This directly improves my clients' ability to manage stress, enhance clarity, and regulate their emotions.

The training I completed taught me over thirty-nine breathing techniques. Having these methods in my toolkit has influenced my life and coaching practice. Functional Breathing exercises can decrease stress, enhance thinking, and balance your nervous system. Practicing Conscious Connected Breathing (CCB) leads to improved energy and emotional well-being.

I make it a point to educate my clients about the science behind breathing. Maintaining the right balance of oxygen and carbon dioxide is crucial for overall well-being. Clients who use techniques like nasal breathing and breath holds have noticed improvements in their thinking and emotions. Some also experienced remarkable transformations in their creative outputs and personal health. Many clients have reported feeling more grounded and concentrated. They found renewed inspiration to face writing difficulties and rediscovering their spiritual connection. It's also common to find solace and guidance through the transformative nature of breath.

Through the practices learnt from Anna's method and other breathwork techniques, I can empower both myself and others to thrive. Breathwork is a powerful tool not just for personal wellness but also for professional success.

Integrating Personal Challenges and Breathwork into Entrepreneurial Success

My journey with breathwork began against a backdrop of personal health challenges. At 18, the doctors diagnosed me with irritable bowel syndrome (IBS). Later on, I had retinal migraines and menopause. The usual treatments didn't help. These experiences led me to a wellness workshop where I first encountered the potential of breathwork. I initially had doubts, but I soon became convinced as I discovered how controlled breathing relieved my symptoms. Breathwork empowered me with a newfound sense of control over my life.

Motivated by my transformation, I felt compelled to share this tool with others facing similar struggles. I felt that starting a wellness business centred on breathwork was the logical next step in my entrepreneurial journey. It aligned with my personal recovery and professional aspirations.

These were my key strategies:

Authentic Marketing

Sharing my journey openly became a key strategy in connecting with my audience. It wasn't just about selling a service; it was about offering an actual solution that had worked for me, one breath at a time.

Targeted Services

I used my personal experiences with IBS, menopause, and mental health challenges to create custom programmes for these issues. This targeted approach helped me attract a dedicated clientele who direly needed these services.

Digital Expansion

By using digital platforms, I increased my reach and started offering virtual sessions that clients could access from anywhere. This flexibility made wellness achievable even for those with the busiest schedules.

Community Building

Building a supportive community was crucial to my business. Clients could share their journeys and successes, creating a healing environment together.

I hope this chapter encourages you to think about how breathwork can impact your personal health challenges and how you can integrate them into your professional life. Taking care of yourself not only helps you grow personally but also builds a thriving business that supports others in overcoming obstacles. The journey of integrating breathwork into my business is not just about entrepreneurship. It proves that the human spirit is resilient and that personal setbacks can lead to professional growth.

Defining Spirituality in Business

I incorporate the principles of spiritual entrepreneurship into my work; blending ancient pagan wisdom with modern business practices. By adopting this unique approach, I can enrich my interactions. Deliver services that reflect integrity, authenticity, and a strong appreciation for the interconnectedness of all living beings.

Aligning business activities with lunar phases and integrating tarot cards and crystals into strategic planning goes beyond symbolism. In business, spirituality extends beyond traditional religious boundaries, emphasising human connection, ethics, and awareness of our interconnected world. It acts as an inner compass, guiding my decisions and valuing more than just profit.

In practice, this means starting every meeting — whether in-person or via Zoom — with a breathwork exercise to centre myself. I also incorporate a short ritual or reflection based on the current Moon phase to set a positive and intentional tone for the day's work. My office also follows these principles, with plants and crystals that create a peaceful and inspiring environment.

Building Relationships Over Sales

Reflecting on my decade-long experience at a high street building society, I cherished the deep rapport built with customers. This connection was not about sales. It involved truly understanding and helping them with important life milestones, like buying a home or preparing for retirement. These relationships were so strong that customers celebrated personal milestones with me, a testament to the trust and bond we had built.

However, when a larger organisation took over, the focus shifted from customer service to sales targets, a change that felt deeply unethical to me. This shift was disillusioning. It led to significant work-related stress, ultimately pushing me to leave and start my business where I could stay true to my ethical compass.

Ethics as a Guiding Light

As a business owner, I choose to operate my enterprise in alignment with my ethics. This means:

☐ There is no pressure from me to buy one of my products, enrol in a course, or join a coaching programme.

☐ I focus on building personal relationships rather than using aggressive sales tactics.

☐ I seek like-minded individuals who share my values for networking and collaborations.

☐ I only support products and companies that I truly trust and have personal experience with. I do this by participating in ambassador programmes and sharing affiliate links.

☐ By maintaining an online community, I can provide free advice to support those who may not have the resources for more extensive help.

Embracing Simplicity and Trusting Intuition

Throughout my career, I've battled the pervasive Fear of Missing Out (FOMO)—the allure of the next big trend or miraculous strategy. Now in my fifties, I've adopted the mantra 'work smarter, not harder'. This doesn't just mean being efficient. It encourages a business model that values balance, wellness, and fulfilment instead of relentless hustle.

This approach deeply aligns with my pagan beliefs, reminding me to respect life's natural rhythms and the importance of self-care. Rather than chasing after every new trend, I've learnt to trust my intuition and make decisions that feel right for me. Nurture relationships with like-minded entrepreneurs and focus on meaningful, sustainable growth.

Moon Phases and Business Rhythms

I intentionally align my business operations with the phases of the Moon. This is not out of superstition, but as a strategic recognition of the natural cycles that influence us all. Let me give you some examples. I take advantage of the full Moon's energy of abundance and manifestation by launching new products or promotions. Conversely, the new Moon, which symbolises new beginnings, is when I focus on setting intentions, planning, and starting new projects. Aligning with lunar cycles helps me use natural energies in my business, improving my planning and execution.

Looking Ahead: The Evolution of Spiritual Entrepreneurship

The more I advance as a breathwork coach, the more I understand the value of incorporating spiritual wisdom into my career. Transitioning from editor to coach has emphasised the significance of flexibility and authenticity. It also highlighted the powerful influence of aligning personal beliefs with one's professional life.

I dedicate this narrative to you and hope this sparks inspiration for you to blend spirituality and entrepreneurship. Together, let's embrace the journey. By committing to live and work authentically, we can overcome various challenges and seize opportunities.

The path of spiritual entrepreneurship is dynamic and ever-evolving, urging us to remain open to continuous learning and adaptation. It calls us to weave our deepest values and spiritual practices into the very fabric of our businesses. To cultivate ventures that thrive while contributing positively to our communities and the greater world.

As this journey unfolds, we remain steadfast in our commitment to authenticity, integrity, and a profound sense of purpose. Each action we take in our professional lives contributes to our personal growth and leads to greater fulfilment and success.

As modern entrepreneurs, we are ready to incorporate eco-friendly practices into our business models. By embracing our responsibility for sustainability, we can contribute to a more aware and empathetic global community.

The combination of ancient pagan wisdom and modern entrepreneurial practices has shaped my ongoing journey. Adding a spiritual essence, the core values of compassion, integrity, and environmental stewardship remain the driving force behind my business.

The story of spiritual entrepreneurship is not ending but unfolding, written with an ink infused with divine essence — a testament to growth, authenticity, and an unwavering commitment to a higher calling.

Meet Kim Brockway

With over 20 years of experience as a pagan practitioner, Kim has cultivated a deep connection to nature and spirituality.

Her pagan journey includes tarot card reading, seasonal celebrations, spell work, and meditation. Kim is an active participant in local pagan gatherings. A deep spiritual connection influences her coaching and editing, leading to a holistic and soulful approach.

Kim is all about empowering women over 40 to chase their writing dreams and find their spiritual paths. She combines her publishing knowledge and love of reading to offer a unique and insightful approach to storytelling. Kim's method includes professional expertise and spiritual wisdom.

Kim firmly believes that everyone has a story to tell, both within the realms of fiction and the tapestry of their spiritual journey. Are you just beginning your writing odyssey, or have you been perfecting your skills for years?

Kim is determined to help you overcome creative blocks. She will help you improve your writing skills by incorporating your spiritual essence into your words. Together, you'll create a novel that fills you with pride and captivates readers far and wide.

Embark on Your Journey to Greater Well-being

Discover the power of breathwork with my complimentary guide, *5 Simple Techniques for Enhanced Well-Being*. This guide helps improve your overall well-being. Learn these breathing exercises that will help you effectively handle stress, sleep well, and achieve balance in your daily life.

These carefully curated techniques offer immediate relief and promote long-term wellness. Let me empower you to navigate life's challenges with ease and clarity.

Download your free guide now and start your journey toward a more serene and centred existence.

https://welcome.wessexwisewoman.co.uk/gift-1

Begin transforming your life today—one breath at a time.

LINKS

Facebook: https://www.facebook.com/WessexWiseWoman/

Instagram: https://www.instagram.com/wessexwisewoman/

Website: https://www.brockwaygatehouse.co.uk/

Chapter Seven

Louise Baines

Embracing the Quirky Path: My Journey into Spiritual Entrepreneurship

L ife is full of surprises and takes us on unexpected journeys. My name is Louise Baines and my journey is a wild ride with funny and profound experiences. I went from daydreaming as a child to becoming a spiritual guide in the business world, proving that embracing your true self can transform you.

Early Spiritual Encounters

As a child, I often found myself lost in the world of my own imagination. Feeling like an outsider amidst the cacophony of playground games and laughter. While my friends revelled in the excitement of tag and hopscotch, I found solace in the quiet whispers of nature, listening intently to the rustling leaves and chirping birds.

It was during these moments of solitude that I first encountered the mystical realm of fairies, pixies, and daydreams. To me, they were not merely figments of imagination, but tangible companions, filling my world with wonder and enchantment. I felt a sense of freedom in their presence, as if I could do anything I desired with their mischievous encouragement.

My cheeky guides, as I fondly called them, were full of joy and spontaneity, urging me to embrace life with reckless abandon. Some may have viewed them as little devils, leading me astray from the path of normalcy. But to me, their presence was a source of pure delight, igniting my curiosity and sense of adventure.

However, as I grew older, I began to feel a sense of unease about my close connection to the spirit world. There came a point where I felt overwhelmed by the intensity of their presence, fearing that I was losing touch with my own humanity. In an effort to regain control, I made the difficult decision to close the door to my spirit guides, retreating into the safety of the mundane world.

Despite this temporary separation, the memories of those early encounters remained etched in my mind. They fuelled my curiosity and shaped my spiritual journey in the years to come. It was through these experiences that I learnt the importance of balance and moderation. I now understand that while the spiritual realm offers boundless freedom, it is essential to remain grounded in my human experience.

Looking back, I am grateful for the lessons learnt during those formative years. They paved the way for me to discover my spiritual side. Though the door to the spirit world may have been closed temporarily, the memories of my cheeky guides continue to inspire me to embrace life with wonder and curiosity. Knowing that the mystical realm will always be there, waiting to welcome me home.

Entrepreneurial Journey

I have been working for the same company since the age of nineteen. I needed money for all my festivals, holidays, and gigs I was going to /on and got a job through an agency. Then I sort of fell into full-time employment. Although I've not always enjoyed the work, I do now. But a job is more than just the tasks and work you do, it's about the people you work with. I've been very lucky that I've always enjoyed working with my colleagues.

It was not until my late thirties that I experienced a profound spiritual awakening, catalysed by a series of cosmic twists and turns. I know everything happens for a reason, but sometimes the reason doesn't become clear until passaging time has given you space and a new perspective.

Amidst bouts of illness and moments of cosmic comedy, I found myself drawn back to the path of spirituality. This massive spiritual awakening brought a newfound clarity and sense of purpose. The experience itself is almost impossible to explain. However, in essence, it was as if someone flipped a light switch, reopening the door to Spirit. It felt the right time.

It was a year of enlightenment, albeit wrapped in the cloak of absurdity. I embraced my calling to integrate spirituality into my personal and professional life. Motivated by a sense of purpose, I began my journey as an entrepreneur, driven by spirituality and self-discovery. Breaking free from the confines of conventional wisdom, I forged my path, fuelled by a desire to share my gifts with the world.

My entrepreneurial journey began with Celestial Wonderland. A spiritual haven where magic, spells, and astrology converged in a tapestry of wonder and enchantment. I created a safe space where people explored the mysteries of the universe and gaining deep knowledge. This allowed forming bonds with like-minded individuals on a journey to find enlightenment. At Celestial Wonderland, you can explore spirituality, find guidance, and connect with like-minded individuals.

As you will read later, it was as I ventured into the realm of entrepreneurship with Celestial Wonderland that my love of crystals grew. I founded a community for people to discover the mystical powers of crystals and connect with like-minded individuals. The Enchanted Crystal Cauldron emerged as a beacon of crystal magic. A nurturing place for those looking to embark on transformative journeys of self-discovery.

These entrepreneurial endeavours are not just business ventures; they are manifestations of my spiritual evolution, embodiments of my quest to integrate spirituality into every facet of my life. As I embraced my true self and honoured my calling, I found fulfilment and purpose in guiding others along the path of spiritual awakening. I've learnt that embracing my true self has been instrumental in my business success. I have worked for the same company for 25 years, but I am determined to make my business my primary source of income. It's through entrepreneurship that I truly found my calling and forged a path illuminated by the radiant light of Spirit.

Unlocking the Mystical Realm: Exploring Crystals in Spiritual Practice

As I reflect on my journey into the captivating world of crystals, I'm reminded of the spark ignited within me during childhood. It was when I first encountered the enchanting allure of an Amethyst. Little did I know then that this simple encounter would blossom into a lifelong passion and a profound spiritual practice.

Crystals have been there for me on my spiritual journey, helping me reflect, heal, and transform. Each crystal in my collection helps me on my life's journey, from Celestite's radiance to Labradorite's whispers.

When it comes to selecting crystals, I trust in the intuitive whispers of my soul. Some crystals beckon to me with their shimmering beauty, while others resonate with a deep, unspoken resonance. Each crystal finds its way into my collection with purpose and intention, enriching my spiritual practice with its unique magic. Whether drawn to the luminous energy of Selenite or the vibrant hues of Citrine.

I have some special crystals, like Celestite and Apophyllite, that I consider my close friends. They help me connect with the archangels and receive spiritual guidance. Labradorite, with its enchanting colours, has become a faithful friend, empowering my intuition and leading me onward. And then there's Selenite, a beacon of purity and light, whose presence brings clarity, protection, and a sense of peace to my surroundings.

I've made crystals a part of my daily routine, bringing their powerful energy into each moment. Having Selenite lamps in my space or wearing crystal jewellery constantly reminds me of the magic that's all around. I use jewellery to balance my mood, and when I need it for the day. For example, every Monday, I wear Moonstone to elevate the Moon energy. If I need motivation, I wear Carnelian to boost my confidence. Crystals are a natural part of my daily routine, bringing purpose and enchantment to everything I do, from meditation to manifestation.

As both a practitioner and a seller of crystals, my mission is to share the transformative power of these mystical gems with others. Through my curated collection and heartfelt guidance, I strive to empower seekers on their own spiritual journey. I offer support, insight, and inspiration every step of the way. I'm proud to guide and protect them on their healing and self-discovery journey, whether in individual sessions or group workshops.

My top eleven must-have gems, each with its own unique enchantment.

- **Clear quartz**. *The master healer* can amplify your intentions and promote clarity.

- **Citrine.** *The joyful sunbeam* invites abundance and positivity into your life.

- **Amethyst.** *The serene guardian* helps you find inner peace and ward off negative energies.

- **Rose quartz**. *The love whisperer* nurtures your heart and relationships.

- **Labradorite**. *The cosmic dreamer* opens doors to your intuition and inner magic.

- **Orange calcite**. *The creativity spark* ignites your artistic passions.

- **Aura quartz.** *The cosmic kaleidoscope* creates a shimmering aura of positivity.

- **Celestite.** *The angel's touch* fosters deep serenity and spiritual connection.

- **Selenite.** *The purity beacon* purifies your space and raises your vibration.

- **Black tourmaline.** *The protective shield* guards against negative energies and psychic attacks.

- **Moonstone.** *The lunar gem* enhances your intuition and feminine energy.

These magical companions are here to uplift, protect, and guide us on our extraordinary journey. Each crystal has its own special powers waiting to enchant your life. Before I despatch any crystal, I cleanse and charge it with an angelic energy of joy, guidance, and love. I hope my knowledge and passion of crystals help elevate a person's life journey.

As I continue to journey deeper into the realm of crystals, I am filled with gratitude for the magic they have brought into my life. Every crystal has a story of healing and transformation, reminding us of our limitless potential. May we continue to walk this path together, weaving enchantment into every moment and embracing the journey with open hearts and curious souls.

Discovering Numerology: A Journey into Hidden Meanings

In 2019, I stumbled upon the captivating world of numerology. It felt like uncovering a hidden treasure chest overflowing with ancient wisdom and cosmic insights. Numerology, for those unfamiliar, is the belief in the mystical relationship between numbers and events. It's a practice that assigns significance to numbers and their vibrations. That these numbers can reveal insights into a person's character, destiny, and even the unfolding of the universe itself.

At first, getting into numerology seemed like going on a solo adventure into the unknown. Friends and family raised eyebrows and thought I was weird for being so obsessed with numbers. They could not understand how much I loved decoding numbers and finding their hidden meanings. But even though everyone doubted me, I stayed determined to uncover the secrets.

Numerology is based on the idea that numbers have specific vibrations that impact individuals and events. Practitioners believe that by interpreting these vibrations and their symbolic meanings, we can gain valuable insights about life. This includes personality traits, relationships, career paths, and even the timing of significant events.

Once I got into numerology, I couldn't resist joining online communities and forums to connect with others who shared my interest. That's where I found a community of people who were all into numbers and sharing their own interpretations. Numerology enthusiasts often use dates and names to calculate and interpret various numerological aspects. By using birth dates, names, or other significant dates, we can calculate life path numbers, destiny numbers, and soul urge numbers.

I connected with like-minded people in online communities who were interested in exploring spirituality. We geeked out over numerology, swapping theories and observations like obsessed fanatics.

Numerology is based on reducing numbers to a single digit and interpreting their meaning, except for master numbers 11, 22, and 33. To achieve this reduction, practitioners commonly use a process known as digit summing or digit reduction. This is where they add the digits of a number together until they get a single digit number.

For example, let's take the birthdate of 15 June, 1985. To calculate the life path number, you would add each digit together: 6 (month) + 1 + 5 (day) + 1 + 9 + 8 + 5 (year) = 35. Then, you'd further reduce this number: 3 + 5 = 8. So, the life path number in this case is 8.

People believe that each single digit number in numerology carries its own unique vibration and meaning. For instance:

1: Represents leadership, independence, innovation, and new beginnings.

2: Signifies cooperation, harmony, balance, and diplomacy.

3: Symbolises creativity, self-expression, communication, and optimism.

4: Reflects stability, practicality, hard work, and traditional values.

5: Represents freedom, adaptability, change, and versatility.

6: Signifies nurturing, responsibility, harmony, and domesticity.

7: Symbolises introspection, spirituality, wisdom, and analytical thinking.

8: Reflects abundance, success, power, and material wealth.

9: Represents compassion, humanitarianism, spiritual enlightenment, and completion.

These interpretations give us an understanding of someone's personality, behaviour, and life.

Master numbers, on the other hand, are considered unique and powerful in numerology because of their heightened vibration and significance. Because they carry a special energy and often require special attention, they do not reduce to a single digit. Master numbers include:

11: Known as the "Master Teacher," representing spiritual illumination, intuition, and enlightenment. People with an 11 life path are often highly intuitive and spiritually gifted.

22: Referred to as the "Master Builder," symbolising mastery, vision, and the ability to manifest dreams into reality. Individuals with a 22 life path are often visionary leaders and builders of large-scale projects.

33: Often called the "Master Healer," representing compassion, guidance, and unconditional love. Those with a 33 life path are believed to have a profound impact on the world through their healing and nurturing abilities.

These master numbers are rare and significant, showing individuals with extraordinary potential and a higher purpose in life. Many people often see them as spiritual guides or mentors, offering wisdom and inspiration to others on their spiritual journey.

Despite the scepticism that still lingered in some corners of my life, I found comfort knowing that I was not alone on my journey. Being around supportive people who got me, I felt empowered to fully dive into my new passion without worrying about the opinions of those who didn't get it.

Numerology offers a unique perspective on life, blending mathematical precision with spiritual insight. It's a tool for self-discovery and personal growth. Numerology helps individuals uncover their strengths, weaknesses, and hidden potentials. By exploring the hidden meaning of numbers, I found validation and a clear sense of purpose.

In the end, my journey into numerology was not just about decoding numbers; it was about finding my place in a world that often felt chaotic and uncertain. Among fellow enthusiasts, I found understanding beyond logic and reason. Numerology opened doors to a deeper understanding of myself and the world around me. It provides a guiding light on my path of self-discovery and spiritual growth.

Astrology: Navigating the Cosmic Symphony

Astrology has been a guiding force in my life since childhood, whispering secrets of the universe and illuminating the path ahead. Since I was a young teenager, horoscopes in teen magazines have fascinated me. While others dismissed them as a load of rubbish, I sensed a deeper resonance, an ancient wisdom echoing through the cosmos.

Throughout my life, astrology has been a constant source of comfort and guidance. It was not until later in life, however, that I heeded the call to delve deeper into the mystical realms of the celestial dance.

My journey into astrology began with a gentle nudge from the Universe, a subtle whisper urging me to explore the cosmic symphony unfolding above. Fascinated by the beautiful patterns in the night sky, I started a journey to understand the hidden messages within.

Every day, I learnt more about astrology and discovered forgotten truths and ancient wisdom. I devoured books, attended workshops, and enrolled in an online course which I passed with distinction. I immersed myself in the language of the stars, seeking to unlock the mysteries of the cosmos.

Through the Moon signs, I discovered a profound connection to the rhythms of the universe, a harmony that echoed through the chambers of my soul. I learnt to navigate the ebb and flow of cosmic energies, harnessing their power to guide me on my journey of self-discovery and spiritual awakening.

Moon signs in astrology refer to the zodiac sign the Moon was in at the time of your birth. Your Sun sign represents your core identity and ego, while your Moon sign reflects your emotional nature and instinctual responses. Knowing your Moon sign can give you valuable insights into your innermost needs, desires, and emotions.

Moon signs represent the position of the Moon in the zodiac at the time of an individual's birth. Every Moon sign has unique qualities that affect our emotions, instincts, and desires.

Here are the basic attributes for each Moon sign:

1. Moon in Aries: Emotionally assertive, impulsive, and independent. People with this placement tend to seek excitement and action, often showing enthusiasm and courage in how they express their emotions.

2. Moon in Taurus: Emotionally stable, sensual, and steadfast. Those with the Moon in Taurus value stability, reliability, and a sense of security in their emotional relationships. They may have a strong attachment to material possessions and enjoy the pleasures of life.

3. Moon in Gemini: Curious, adaptable, and communicative. Those with this placement may experience fluctuating emotions and a need for mental stimulation. They enjoy variety and may express their emotions through communication and social interactions.

4. Moon in Cancer: Nurturing, sensitive, and intuitive. Individuals with this placement have strong emotional connections to family and home. They are highly empathetic, but may experience mood swings. They desire emotional security and stability in their relationships.

5. Moon in Leo: Dramatic, generous, and expressive. Those who have this placement tend to seek validation by engaging in creative activities and taking on leadership roles. They hope to be acknowledged and admired. They may have a strong need for self-expression and may be emotionally expressive and generous.

6. Moon in Virgo: Practical, analytical, and detail-oriented. Those with this placement may have a tendency to over-analyse their emotions, seeking perfection and order in their emotional lives. They may express their feelings through acts of service and attention to detail.

7. Moon in Libra: Harmonious, diplomatic, and relationship-oriented. Individuals with this placement value balance and fairness in their emotional connections. They may seek harmony in their relationships and may have a strong desire for partnership and cooperation.

8. Moon in Scorpio: Intense, passionate, and secretive. People with this placement deeply experience emotions and may feel drawn to the mysteries of life and death. They may have a strong need for emotional depth and intimacy in their relationships.

9. Moon in Sagittarius: Optimistic, adventurous, and philosophical. Those with this placement value freedom and independence in their emotional expression. They may seek emotional fulfilment through travel, learning, and exploring new ideas.

10. Moon in Capricorn: Ambitious, disciplined, and reserved. Individuals with this placement may strongly need to control and structure in their emotional lives. They are practical and responsible, seeking emotional security through hard work and achievement.

11. Moon in Aquarius: Unconventional, humanitarian, and progressive. People with this placement value individuality and innovation in their emotional expression. Independence might be very important to them, and they express their emotions by participating in social activism and community work.

12. Moon in Pisces: Imaginative, compassionate, and intuitive. Those with this placement are highly sensitive and may have psychic abilities. They are likely to be very empathetic and find comfort in being creative, spiritual, and helping others.

For example, if your Moon is in Pisces, like mine, you may be deeply intuitive, empathetic, and sensitive to the feelings of others. You may have a rich inner life, filled with vivid dreams, fantasies, and creative imaginings. However, you may also struggle with boundaries, as you absorb the energy and emotions of those around you, sometimes to your own detriment.

On the other hand, if your Moon is in a more grounded sign like Taurus, you may have a strong need for stability, security, and comfort. Delighting in the small things, like yummy food, lovely scenery, and pleasurable sensations, can bring you happiness. However, you may also be prone to stubbornness and resistance to change, as you prefer to stick with what feels familiar and safe.

Knowing your Moon sign can also shed light on how you process and express your emotions. For instance, if your Moon sign is Aries, you may be prone to quick anger but also quick forgiveness. Whereas if your Moon sign is Virgo, you may express your emotions in a reserved manner but show deep devotion through practical acts of service.

In my case, being a Moon in Pisces, I enjoy doing creative activities, practicing spirituality, and being in nature. I also feel a deep sense of compassion and empathy for others, often putting their needs above my own. By embracing my Moon sign qualities, I can tap into my intuition, imagination, and emotional depth. This guides me on my journey of self-discovery and spiritual entrepreneurship.

Astrology serves as a guiding light in my business, revealing the path ahead and helping me understand the cosmic currents that impact us. I launch new ventures on auspicious astrological dates, aligning my actions with the celestial forces at play. Connecting with the cosmos empowers me to navigate the unpredictable journey of entrepreneurship gracefully.

By using astrology, I can adapt my services to match each client's unique astrological profile. By considering their birth charts and planetary alignments, I can offer personalised guidance and support. This helps them navigate life's challenges with clarity and confidence.

In essence, astrology is more than just a tool for divination; it is a profound and sacred language, a reflection of the divine order woven into the fabric of existence. By embracing its wisdom, we can unlock the secrets of the universe and embark on a unique journey of self-discovery and spiritual growth.

I am filled with gratitude for the wisdom and guidance astrology has given upon me. May its light continue to illuminate my path and guide me on my journey of self-discovery and spiritual awakening.

Unlocking Wisdom: Journeying with Oracle Cards

I began my journey with oracle cards back in 2019. It all started when I sought guidance from other spiritual practitioners, and each time, the message seemed to echo the same sentiment: 'You know what to do. You can do it.' It was as if the Universe was nudging me to explore the world of oracle cards myself.

So, I decided to take the leap and purchased my first oracle deck, the beautiful *Moonology* Oracle deck, by Yasmin Boland. Drawn to its enchanting imagery and deep symbolism, I eagerly delved into the world of lunar wisdom and intuitive guidance. Little did I know that this initial step would unlock the door to a vast realm of spiritual insight and profound connection. I immersed myself in the *Moonology* Oracle deck. I discovered the power of tapping into the cyclical energy of the Moon phases and harnessing its transformative influence in my readings.

Since then, my collection has expanded. Each new deck adding its own unique essence and perspective to my practice. I love my fairies and Devine animal decks, but there are many available to suit all tastes. For example, the *Wild Unknown* oracle deck, known for its captivating artwork and powerful symbolism. Each card in this deck offers a glimpse into the depths of the subconscious and invites self-analysis and self-discovery.

Another popular deck is the *Sacred Rebels* oracle deck, which celebrates the spirit of nonconformity and empowerment. With its bold imagery and provocative messages. This deck serves as a catalyst for embracing authenticity and embracing your true self.

Angelic guidance and divine wisdom infuse the *Angel Answers'* oracle cards. These cards always provide messages of hope and inspiration, whether you need guidance or encouragement.

Oracle cards have helped me connect with my spiritual guides, who assist me in interpreting the cards and giving guidance to others. Each reading is a sacred exchange of energy, where intuition and insight converge to illuminate the path ahead.

For me, oracle cards are not just tools for divination; they're portals to the soul, offering profound insights and guidance for navigating life's twists and turns. Oracle cards have become an important part of my spiritual practice, helping me find clarity, inspiration, and empowerment.

Expanding Spiritual Influence in Business

In my journey as an entrepreneur infused with spirituality, every facet of my business reflects my deep connection to the spiritual realm. I don't just provide services; I create safe spaces for people to explore their spirituality, find comfort, and awaken their inner light.

I believe in a holistic approach to business, where I seamlessly integrate spirituality into every aspect. From the way I communicate with clients to the energy I infuse into my workspace, spirituality permeates everything I do. By considering the complete picture, I can nurture an environment that supports personal and professional development.

Central to my business philosophy are ethical principles rooted in spirituality. Honesty, integrity, and compassion guides my interactions with clients. This ensures that I infuse every engagement with authenticity and sincerity. By upholding these values, I foster trust and cultivate meaningful connections with those I serve.

My services go beyond conventional transactions; they are soulful offerings designed to uplift and inspire. My goal is to assist individuals in having transformative experiences, embracing their true selves, and feeling empowered. I do this through intuitive readings, spiritual coaching, and transformative workshops.

At the heart of my business is a vibrant community of seekers and dreamers united by a shared quest for spiritual growth. I run events, gatherings, and online forums. I nurture a welcoming environment where people can connect, support one another, and share their experiences. Working within this community magnifies the effect of my work, inspiring positive change and transforming us as a whole.

While I navigate the changing world of entrepreneurship, I am dedicated to constantly evolving and growing. Taking inspiration from spiritual teachings and divine guidance, I change my strategies and offerings to meet the evolving needs of my clients and community. This commitment to evolution helps my business stay adaptable and up-to-date.

Besides my own success, I aim to motivate others to embark on their own journeys of self-discovery and spiritual awakening. My stories inspire others to embrace their power and reach their full potential.

At the core of my mission is a deep desire to spread light and love to all who cross my path. I aim to bring positivity wherever I go. Whether it's through small acts of kindness, meaningful conversations, or life-changing experiences. In this way, I strive to be a beacon of hope and inspiration in a world that needs healing and renewal.

As I follow my path as an entrepreneur with a spiritual approach, I am grateful for the chance to help and inspire others. With each step forward, I remain guided by the wisdom of the divine, trusting in the unfolding of my path and the limitless potential of the human spirit.

Inviting You to the Mystical Realms: Embrace Your Spiritual Journey

Within Celestial Wonderland and The Enchanted Crystal Cauldron, I infuse every aspect with spirituality. From my daily rituals to my interactions with clients. Through intuitive readings and spiritual guidance, I offer a beacon of light for those navigating their own paths of self-discovery. My ethical principles and spiritual practices serve as guiding lights, illuminating the way forward for those who seek my wisdom.

My journey has been marked by challenges. These hurdles have tested my resolve and shaped me as an entrepreneur and spiritual guide. Yet, it is through these challenges that I have discovered my true strength and resilience. By staying true to myself and my spiritual values, I have navigated the twists and turns of the entrepreneurial path with grace and courage.

I see my business growing in the future because I am dedicated to spiritual principles. I envision a future where my work reaches even greater heights, touching the lives of countless souls in need of guidance and inspiration.

Through my daily rituals and practices, I remain steadfast in my dedication to my spiritual journey and the impact it has on those around me.

Beyond my immediate business goals, I see my journey and experiences as a contribution to the broader community of seekers and dreamers. I hope that by sharing my story and being authentic, I can inspire others to embark on their own journeys of self-discovery and spiritual awakening. Through my work, I seek to create a ripple effect of positive change, spreading light and love to all who cross my path.

Weaving every twist and turn into my life's tapestry, embracing my true self, led me to spiritual entrepreneurship. Despite the ups and downs, I've stayed true to my spiritual values and commitment to being genuine. I'm committed to guiding and inspiring others on their spiritual journeys as I navigate my path with strength and confidence. Together, let us embark on a journey of self-discovery and spiritual awakening, spreading light and love to all who cross our paths.

Step into the magical realms of Celestial Wonderland and The Enchanted Crystal Cauldron, where sacred wonders await. Explore, discover, and connect with us as we illuminate the path to spiritual awakening and empowerment. Join our community and let your journey begin.

Meet Louise Baines

Celestial Witch and Spiritual Entrepreneur

I'm Louise, your guide through the enchanted realms of energy and spirituality. With a passion for spreading light and weaving magic, I've dedicated myself to empowering others on their mystical journeys. With my background as a lightworker and entrepreneur, I create transformative experiences for those looking for deeper connections with themselves and the Universe.

Join me as we embark on an extraordinary adventure, where dreams manifest and possibilities abound. As a spiritual entrepreneur, I combine intuition and practical advice to help you navigate life's trials genuinely and gracefully.

With a background rooted in the mystical arts and a heart open to endless possibilities, I invite you to explore the depths of your soul, unlock your innate magic, and embrace the wonder of the unknown. Together, let's illuminate the path ahead, infusing every moment with light, love, and boundless wonder.

Welcome to the journey of a lifetime, where miracles unfold, and the celestial dances in harmony with the earthly. I'm honoured to be your companion on this sacred voyage of self-discovery and transformation.

With love and light,

Louise, Your Celestial Witch, and Spiritual Guide

LINKS

Facebook: https://www.facebook.com/celestialwond

Instagram: https://www.instagram.com/louise.spiritualmentor/

Chapter Eight

Rachael Hall

The Wealth Ascension Awakening

Disclaimer – the information contained in this chapter is meant to provide insights into financial planning and should not be construed as financial advice. Financial Planning should be personalised to each individual and there will be many more considerations than those addressed in this chapter alone.

A Baptism of Fire (excerpt from the book "Fearless Connection")

*I*t's 2003, and I'm standing in the bar of a London hotel. The smell of stale beer fills the air, and I'm wondering whether anyone would notice if I added a shot of vodka to the Diet Coke I've just ordered - I decide against it as it'll probably just make me even more tired. My feet are aching from the new shoes I bought for the conference, and I've got a caffeine headache, having spent all day knocking back cups of coffee, so I have the energy to help out at this event. Who'd have thought

153

handing out brochures, registering people and ushering delegates into stuffy conference rooms to watch fund managers give financial presentations could be this tiring? We are now waiting for the CEO to give the final address, so we can wrap up for the day.

Finally, the conference room doors open and we can hear the rumble of people leaving the room. A group of fifteen men head straight for the bar. Lumbering across the hotel lobby like a herd of geriatric elephants, they look at me and comments are exchanged which, thankfully, I can't make out. One man makes a beeline for me with a smirk on his face. Before I even realise what's going on, he lifted me up and announces to the group, "I want to have sex with you!". He squeezes me hard and I feel myself turn bright red. Now, I'm angry. I do not react well to humiliation.

"Sorry ... I'm not into Necrophilia", is my reply.

He drops me and a look of embarrassment sweeps over his chubby reddening face as the rest of the group of men burst into laughter. He apologises, although more to himself for his bruised ego than to me and any sense of shame as to the inappropriateness of his actions.

This was my introduction to the world of financial services, and has no doubt acted as a springboard to a career that has been characterised by successfully challenging stereotypes to become a recognised leader in my industry.

I can thank my strong northern upbringing and matriarchal grandmother for my inner strength and resilience. It's sad to say this, but back then my 23-year-old self, probably didn't think this was such a big deal, because "pervy men" in pinstripe suits were more or less an everyday irritation that had to be dealt with in the world of financial services.

Of course, not all the men were like that, but the patriarchy saw to it, if they were to show any degree of empathy towards a woman, that was a sign of 'weakness' and they were very much considered being bottom of the pecking order. The odd one would roll their eyes at me in a supportive way and whisper "good on you" but only when the prime offenders were no longer in earshot.

So these are the origins of the quick-talking, self-reliant, and successful woman I now see when I look in the mirror. This is the energy I have been required to develop and still carry with me — a suit of armour and a double-edged sword. It has created both opportunity and isolation in equal measure.

Fast forward twenty years from that first conference. Having juggled misogyny, motherhood, and inner doubt, I now have a business which is scaling with high levels of year-on-year growth, one year which reached the dizzy heights of nearly 600%. Most coaches would have you believe that this is living the dream, but they rarely share the ugly truths. Don't get me wrong, this can be a thoroughly rewarding period of time and I do feel proud of where I am at today — I have a national reputation as a specialist in my field, have three-month waiting lists for people wanting to join our programmes, and I feel nothing but gratitude for that level of recognition and the trust that people place in me and my team; but, that said, a scaling business is a fast-moving and cash hungry monster. If it doesn't get fed, this little beast will bite back with such ferocity that it can make you question whether it's all worth it.

You may find yourself navigating burnout and experience panic attacks every time you hit new levels of income. Costs increase and as you hire more staff, you will likely find yourself feeling the pressure and questioning every decision you make. Solopreneurs soon find themselves managing teams of people, a role which they never expected and for which they have no experience. Dealing with many different personality types can be overwhelming, especially if you don't hire the right people.

So, if you are reading this chapter and find yourself in this position today, congratulations! You have done amazingly well to get where you are. What I want to share with you today is my spiritual journey and how my awakening impacted my life and business, how I navigated this process to transform my practice into something new, pioneering changes which should serve to positively impact our planet and our clients lives for the greatest good.

As great as it was to be the tough talking, hard-hitting corporate career woman, I was also stuck in the toxic masculine for many years. Working within such a male dominated industry turned me into the ice queen, because at the time I believed this to be the optimum way to show up for work. While it may have helped me climb the career ladder it also had me locked into the toxic masculine, and after being put in a position where I could have potentially sued one company for maternity discrimination and another for constructive dismissal, I decided I had had enough of employment and formed my own company.

Having children softened me, but I coasted in and out of burnout. Raising children and running a business has its merits, but also can be intense. As Annabel Crabb says, *"the obligation for working mothers is a very precise one: the feeling that one ought to work as if one did not have children, while raising one's children as if one did not have a job".*

The situation was somewhat exacerbated when I became a personality in the NHS Pension world of Twitter (or X as it's now called). In 2018, a Twitter storm had erupted about a form of tax doctors were paying on their pensions, which had a catastrophic effect on NHS services.

To avoid these tax charges, doctors had to earn less money, which essentially meant cancelling clinics and refusing to work the waiting lists. This problem was nationwide and it couldn't have happened at a worse time, shortly before the pandemic hit.

This particular form of tax was a complex beast and a lot of professionals didn't understand it. Fortunately for me, I had been studying it for many years and, unbeknownst to me, at that point in time, I was the country's leading expert. Little did I know that my sharp tongue and tenacity would propel me onto a national stage.

Before long, I was being quoted in the mainstream news, even being invited onto the Martin Lewis show at one point, although by the team we responded to the producer, the position had already been filled. Being northern has its advantages, and one is being able to take a very complex topic and making it really easy to understand.

I led a movement with a few others, which successfully lobbied the UK government to change the tax system — eventually they did. I was pleased to say that while there are still ongoing disputes about doctors' pay and pensions, I really felt like we made a difference. It was a job well done.

My Spiritual Awakening

I would never have described myself as particularly "spiritual" or religious for that matter, I always considered myself to be the complete opposite, because I love physics and thought experiments like Schrodinger's Cat, string theory, and quantum entanglement. Over the years, my view of the world has broadened, especially since the Pandemic, which felt so surreal it was like living in a movie. Since then I've been utterly convinced that there is another realm of science and physics yet to be discovered which can explain many of the experiences we have, which we currently label as "supernatural".

In the world of evolution, who knows where we will be 100 years from now, so far be it from me to deny another person's truth? To be honest, I've never been concerned with other people's beliefs and always been so respectful of religion as I have a diverse portfolio of clients with different cultural backgrounds. One of my absolute favourite places on Earth is Iceland and according to National Geographic, over 54% of the population believe in Elves, who are even represented by a member of parliament! The way I see it is that no person has the right to judge another when we are all believing in things that can not be scientifically be proven in one way or another.

So when I proverbially "woke up" it was like a sudden shock to the system and it felt so uncomfortable that I longed to go back to sleep again. But once you see or experience a sudden awakening, you can't go back, you can't "unsee" it and you have to find a way to live with it. I imagine this is how people feel when they have a Near Death Experience. I know that there are support groups for people who have had these encounters, but unfortunately, there was nothing like this for me when I had my blindfold ripped off. So I've decided to share some of my experiences in the hope that this will one day this will be someone else's survival guide.

For me, Channelling is just an expansion of consciousness, which we are usually discouraged not to use out of fear that we are just "Imagining things" or "daydreaming". However, we do take notice of our dreams and may often discuss them among friends who often like to work out the psychological meaning or symbology. So why do we think this can only be done in sleep states and not whilst we are conscious? In my very humble opinion, we just haven't explored this well enough to feel confident discussing amongst ourselves.

When we rest into meditation and allow our minds to wander in complete confidence that THIS IS OK AND WE ARE NOT GOING MAD we can learn a lot about ourselves, as I did when I started journalling after meditation. I've found the images, words or messages that I receive insightful, always helping me to learn more about myself or navigate situations in life. Whether you believe we are accessing parts of our sub-conscious that we haven't before, or if they are coming from the divine, it really doesn't matter, as long as you feel in control and that this process is adding value to your life whilst you continue to thrive.

I do believe that we are all inextricably linked and that there are many physicists like Einstein and Nicholas Tesla, along with psychiatrists, such as like Carl Jung, who would support this view. I also believe that modern physics is very much in alignment with some spiritual beliefs, even if it's just theory. So, I think these practices should be explored and encouraged if it's adding value to your life.

There is so much inner wisdom that we can access with so much ease and grace and we don't even know it yet!

In The Beginning

I was juggling being a mum and the owner of a business experiencing such a phenomenal pace of growth, so I wanted to explore different wellbeing practices that would help me improve my energy levels. I had heard of Reiki and liked that it was a complete contrast to working within a very scientific industry, such as financial services.

My first Reiki session went really smoothly. I didn't have any major breakthroughs, but I could certainly feel a movement in energy, which was strange. At the end, the Reiki Master told me she had found and cleared a metallic band over my third eye, which was preventing me from using it and that it was highly likely I had been a spiritual leader in a previous life. I had never really heard anything like it, but then having just came out of the Pandemic, I had never experienced anything like that either, so I just ran with it. At the time, my personal view was that she was probably just feeling into the Botox injections I'd had a few weeks earlier!

But the idea of reincarnation fascinated me. From being a child, I used to ponder over the cycle of life and death, convinced that it was just like the water cycle; water was life, evaporation was death, clouds were heaven, and the rain was birth. I used to think ghosts were just clouds in the sky because our bodies are mainly made up of water. These days I tell my children that they are made from stars because that is science fact, but as an abstract concept, I am rather fond of my 5-year-old science fiction!

Rachael Hall

Past Life Regression

When anyone talked about their earliest memory, my mind would always return to this memory but still to this day my mum swears it cannot be true because we never visited anywhere with a room like this — and yet I remember it so vividly! An old Victorian bedroom with a marble fireplace and a large mahogany fourposter bed. I distinctly remember running my hands over the green satin sheets and admiring the fireplace. Wanting to explore this memory in more detail, I agreed to return to have a past life regression; thinking that it would be an interesting experience, if nothing else. The only intention I had prior to the session was to make sense of this "memory".

When I arrived for the past life regression, we had a pre-session discussion. She noted down some questions that I wanted answers to and informed me that I would be under hypnosis for no longer than an hour. Unfortunately for me, the session didn't exactly go as planned. We never returned to the Victorian period, instead we landed in Atlantis and it was all Mermaids, before feeling like I had been attacked and lifted off the bed after I was shot off at lightning speed into the cosmos!

She spent most of the session asking my sub-conscious what she should do about her business, life, and projects, then used me for remote viewing purposes. In total, the session lasted 4.5 hours and was finally shut down by a spirit guide who I saw standing in a waterfall of blue energy. They helped me wake up, and I was able to get myself home. With hindsight, I should have reported her, but I just never wanted to open that up and spent the next 12 months of my life healing from that experience.

You would be forgiven for thinking it would put me off Reiki for life, but it didn't because I understand not everyone is like that. After having a vision of Archangel Michael in my mind's eye during my friends Reiki session I was attuned to Reiki degree 1 & 2. I had no intention of ever practicing this professionally, but I often use it on my children and found it an important aspect of my spiritual development.

Awakenings

The encounter with the past life regression was the catalyst of what can only be described as a colossal awakening. I had some supernatural experiences when I was younger — once seeing a ghost — but nothing like this. It all began early 2023, and I remember the day because I took the dogs for a walk in the park and in my mind's eye, I could see 3 figures surrounding me in white robes. I just couldn't shake it off, so I allowed it to just sit with me for a while. Later that day, we drove to Snowdonia and in that same week I stopped eating meat, which was not a conscious decision; I just couldn't bring myself to do it.

I later learned later from my amazing friend and Numerologist Jo Soley, that I had hit my Year 11 March 2023, which is meant to be a very spiritual year. Jo couldn't have been more accurate because this really was a year like no other! I would often wake up in the mornings with a sudden knowing or revelation about a situation I was dealing with. I was also experiencing lucid dreams. One I will never forget was when I found myself stood in a shopping mall with a man dressed in white, who looked lost and confused. We started to transfer energy through our hearts, and I think this was some sort of healing. When I woke the next day, I found his face in my news feed. I couldn't believe it! He had been reported as a missing person, but I knew he was dead and that he was surrounded by brown water. Later that day, my fear was confirmed, and they did actually find his body at the bottom of a river.

I then woke up out of one dream and dropped into another state where you're fully alert but not actually awake. I could hear a girl crying in my room and I just knew that she had had a traumatic death. It really did freak me out and the next day I just sat and asked for all of these experiences to stop, which they did.

At the time, I didn't know anything at all about grounding or protection practices and I don't think I would have taken anyone seriously even if they had told me, because believe it or not I was still doubting these experiences, writing them off as dreams.

Whilst the visitations of dead people stopped, they were suddenly replaced by other people which the spiritual community would refer to as "ascended masters" but the messages were messy and I couldn't make head nor tail of what was going on, other than there were references to past lives. But they just didn't slow down, and I was finding it hard to deal with, because I was waking up exhausted and often upset.

At the end of one yoga session, whilst in Shavasana I received a sudden image of an Asian man sat on a rock. I pondered over whether this was Shiva and assumed that it was confirmation when the image changed to a close up of his face. I'm sure this would freak any normal person out, but I felt comfortable with him. I started connecting with him quite regularly in my meditation and he introduced to me to a channel called "the Garden of Eden". It was a safe place that I could retreat to when I was overwhelmed with all the images, stories, and messages. This place was a large Victorian walled garden that had a huge pink rose bush in the corner and a stream of running water. I found this visualisation really peaceful and I would often imagine sleeping underneath the rose bush with an Atlantean spirit guide keeping watch. If I ever had nightmares, he would come in and pull me out, which only really ever happened twice.

Whether you are a sceptic or not, what I feel this experience taught me was a method of relaxation and deep peace, which I was able to tap into fully conscious or in a sleep state. I don't tend to use it now, but it was useful for me at a time when I did not know about grounding and protection practices, so in a way I invented my own!

Retreats

Not everything I have encountered can be explained by daydreams. In fact, the following is probably one of the strangest experiences I have ever had. One of my good friends, Ali Knight, runs the most amazing retreats. In 2023, she happened to be holding one in a beautiful village called Rhoscolyn in Wales. The house in Rhoscolyn has the most amazing views of Mount Snowdon and the whole place feels magical.

There were seven of us on the retreat and we spent the weekend journalling, working on ourselves as well as our business. One day, we had been for a hike and sea swimming and when we returned to the house; we sat around the dinner table chatting amongst ourselves, waiting for dinner. Suddenly, I felt a huge vibration sweep over my body. My heart was pounding in my chest and I felt like I was going to have a panic attack. I knew something was up and so I made my excuses and went for a lie down in the sitting room on my own.

When I closed my eyes and had an instant knowing that I was not alone. I could feel someone called Isis, who I knew was Egyptian, but very little else. She told me I was going to receive a scared protection. I shook it off, thinking I had clearly overdone things that day and was experiencing a panic attack.

When I got up and left the room, I closed the door and felt a searing pain shoot across my abdomen. My period had arrived. Not unusual, you may think, but I was mid-cycle (always regular) and definitely not peri-menopausal. The period lasted 48 hours.

I've never had anything like it before or ever since, at the age of 43. A year later, I learned that this is a phenomenon which can occur when people visit her temple in Egypt. Still, to this day, I have no idea why that happened to me, but it did, and that is my truth. Make of it what you will.

Astrology & Metaphors

When I started reading over the notes in my journal, I noticed that they sometimes had astrological significance. I first noticed this when I started noticing some of the images centred around roses and Venus. Venus orbits in a rose formation, so it wasn't difficult to work that one out, but these first came to me at a time when Venus was changing its astrological position. Then I received a very clear message I was going to receive a gift that it would be in the form of a Pleiadian Rose. I'm not sure what I thought at the time, possibly that it would be like the Next Delivery or an "inter-galactic-flora" bouquet would be delivered to me from an "unknown sender"! Sadly, the flowers never did arrive, but later that year I was at a workshop where someone referred to a meditation called "Pleiadian Rose" which I found interesting.

Expanding My Community

During this time, I had the advantage of being married to a psychiatrist and I would occasionally share these experiences with my husband, often asking if I was losing my mind!

Clearly, my husband had no idea what I was talking, and he never experienced anything remotely supernatural in his life, but I'll give him his due: He would never belittle me or ask me to stop. In fact, if anything, he fully supported me and encouraged me to explore it, often calling me "fearless". In a way that grounded me and gave me the courage to continue with these exercises.

In a way, he taught me that it was OK to have spiritual experiences, as long as I stayed grounded and was happy and thriving. It wasn't always fun and games, but I always centred and he always helped me to keep an open mind. So, I journalled and tracked these thought patterns in an attempt to learn more about myself, whilst also trying to identify and dispel any self-limiting patterning or beliefs.

My non-spiritual friends persevered with me, but really, there are only so many times you can mention being woken up at 3 am by Mount Snowdown to tell you a portal was open, without them staring back at you with a blank look. I wondered how I was ever going to be accepted by my existing community and so I hid these experiences from my family and friends for a long time.

As I write these words, some of the people that I never thought would be accommodating to these experiences have shown the most interest. Some are now taking their first steps into the world of spirituality, accessing modalities such as breathwork or meditation, which we know is a great approach to mindfulness practice.

But in the beginning, none of my community spoke about chakras, let alone channelling. Many of them practised yoga but didn't really talk about anything spiritual and I often felt like I had been marooned on a spiritual desert island and longed to go home. But I couldn't. I had changed, but everyone else around me was still the same. It was painful; it made me feel really isolated and lonely. Perhaps that was the symbology behind me lying underneath the rose bush with only a spirit guide for company, who knows, but it was uncomfortable and I had changed. I knew I was a different person and the only way through to the other side was to find people like me.

I knew it was time to expand my network in search of the "truth". I'm not sure what "truth" I was searching for, but I wanted reassurance that others were having similar experiences to me and that this was just a "new normal". The problem was that I had never been involved with any spiritual or religious communities before. I had no network to engage with at all. I didn't know where to start or what to read.

Through the online coaching community, I eventually found Kelly Vikings. With Kelly's help, I finally started to find my feet and learned about grounding, clearing, and protection practices. Kelly taught me about the energetic circuitry running through our bodies called "Human Design" and I felt less lonely because she was able to validate my experiences, often receiving the same messages as me before I even spoke them out loud during our sessions.

Akashic Record Clearing

Finally, my network was expanding, and I started to connect with others who were going through their own journeys, but there was something that was still not quite right and I couldn't put my finger on it.

The past lives stories and my thirst for the truth were driving me mad and I wanted to make sense of them all. When I look back now, I would refer to this period as being stuck in the "karmic plughole": A mixture of half-truth and distortion, which just needs clearing. I had heard about Akashic Records and found a two-day workshop in Glastonbury that taught how to clear your own Akashic Records. Adrian Lee, an energy healer and expert in the Akashic Records and Melissa Connor, a quantum healer and spiritual mentor, ran it. I now use Adrian's meditations weekly and Melissa has mentored me on and off for a while now. I cannot thank them enough because I found them at a time when it couldn't have been more needed.

The clearing on day one was so intense that we all felt completed drained. That night, I fell into bed and didn't move until the next day. But day two was nothing short of magical. Golden light flooded my third eye, making it difficult for me to see. I was told that my heart was being wrapped in golden light too, and I finally felt like I had landed.

That weekend, someone captured an image of three suns above the Glastonbury Hills. So beautiful. In fact, that weekend proved to be such a hit that it didn't end there. When I returned home and mentioned to friends and family what I had been doing, I had half expected it to be written off as mumbo jumbo, but instead, everyone was lining up for a session!

Over the next two weeks, I would perform clearings on seventeen people, including a group clearing on a retreat. Well, the universe obviously had plans for me and I was just along for the ride. By this point, I just decided to surrender and flow!

Shadow Work

During this time, I changed as a person. I questioned who I was and why on earth I was working in such a materialistic industry. I initially wanted to run for the hills, but I knew I had a lot to give and despite the spiritual madness, I was absolutely ablaze with work. My clients were having real wins and breakthroughs. They were yielding significant results.

We were retiring people ten years earlier than they thought possible and one of my clients was awarded a £62,500 tax write off using the quantum calculations in my expert witness report. There was no suggestion at all that this wasn't where I was meant to be. The exact opposite; I was making positive changes to people's lives.

So, in an attempt to find balance, I took the decision to start on the shadow work everyone always talks about, which would help me with the next part of my journey.

This time, I started to work on rebalancing feminine and masculine energies. I have to say that this work has completely changed me as a person. Once I started to being able to recognise narratives of a "toxic masculine" or a "wounded feminine" nature, I would clear, rebalance, release, and move forward.

Instead of wanting to run away and live on a farm in the country, I felt ready to pioneer change within my industry and others. I accepted that the reason I found myself in financial services in the first place, was to change the industry from Wolf of Wall Street to one of Financial Freedom and Sovereignty, for all our clients.

I had finally found the joy in my work again and I had a new business partner, who was very much on the same page as me. I realised that together we could create something special and something which reflected our values and could yield extremely positive results for our clients and the planet, at the same time.

Business Mentoring

Catherine Morgan was my business mentor for just over a year and helped me through this period of my life. She introduced me to her amazing community of women who are now really close to me. I suddenly realised that there were lots of women going through the same journey as me, but we were all experiencing this in different ways. We often get stuck riding the toxic masculine hamster wheel until one day we wake up and realise we've changed, but the business hasn't.

Rather than focusing on the money, profit, and turnover, we were questioning what impact we were having on the world and whether we were truly aligned with our values.

At the same time, I was struggling to come to terms with the new version of myself — the shift into spirituality was not always a comfortable one — Catherine and her community gave me the courage and confidence to be me. Instead of calling me weird, this community held me in its arms and told me I was safe. They celebrated and supported me during my transformation, and so did my amazing friend and colleague, Charlotte Ritchie. She has been my rock, showing nothing but dedication and loyalty to both me, the business, and our clients.

Surrounding yourself with the right people is critical to your mental health and wellbeing. Never underestimate the power of your community. That's why I've honoured so many of them in my chapter; I value the contributions that they have made to my life and work, whilst I have been on this journey and without them, I wouldn't be where I am today. I also wouldn't have met my new business partner Emma Wright, a part of this community, who has also been on her own spiritual journey. Together, we are focused on changing the industry for the better and promoting financial sovereignty for all.

Ascension

The spiritual community loves to talk about Ascension. I have had no training in this at all, but I do believe that this is what I have been experiencing when I read about it. To me, *Ascension is an expansion of consciousness and the creation of new manifestations.* I also think ascension is about becoming fully conscious and embodied more than we ever have been in our lives. We can do this by using practices we have been told are "mumbo jumbo", but are actually really useful once you get over the pain threshold. These *new manifestations* often require us to rebalance *new energies* by finding a way to harmonise female and masculine energy.

The New Earth (5D)

I'm no expert on this concept, but I do have a view on it. Firstly, that if everyone celebrated our differences, the world would be a more peaceful place. So with that in mind, we should have the space to create our own version of the world around us. Therefore, I would hope that we ultimately get to decide what this "new earth" looks like, in ways that are joyous and comfortable for us personally. Not everyone wants spaceships parking themselves on the lawn, but I do think most people want to experience love and joy.

Frequency Adjustments

Frequency adjustments are simply changes in your energy levels, which I call Frequency Adjustments. This process is challenging, but there are some things that I did or values I returned to, which made life a little easier. I will share these with you:

Switch off the news. It's a narrative, not always fact, although some channels are better than others, but journalists don't always get it right. That said, you should always remain aware of the world around you.

Stay in the heart and act in good grace. Maintain strong boundaries. Remember, you belong to you.

Truth and integrity. Don't preach what you don't practice. Are you really in alignment with your values?

Laughter. Find your joy and don't be so serious. When things get heavy, simply change the frequency: laugh, sing, dance and don't forget to play.

The Void. People talk about the dreaded "void" and this is when you feel lost and like you have no direction or that your spirit guides have abandoned you. I always found this a really useful process to shed what doesn't serve you and act as a portal of creation which enables you to rebirth into something more magical. I also think we can get too hung up or reliant on the external when we need to inward and basically fall in love with ourselves again. In my opinion, this is a very important part of this journey and shouldn't be feared or avoided at all.

Release: do not carry other people's negative beliefs and thought forms. If you spend all day processing someone else's energy, you cannot truly know yourself. Spend time getting to know who YOU are and not manifesting other people's truths as your own. Never forget: You belong to you.

Don't be afraid of your dark. Do the shadow work. Identifying self-limiting beliefs will help you break negative cycles. You *do* have the power to change and we do not need to be defined by — what we consider to be — our mistakes.

"Candle blower-outers". I owe this phrase to Brene Brown, who talks about the importance of surrounding ourselves with people who value and protect our light, not extinguish it. Fear seeding and negativity should be avoided. Use your discernment. Put yourself on a social media detox if, and when, needed!

Through my experiences, I've discovered that when the universe is onside, you'll experience synchronicities. You'll have been told "it's just a coincidence" but don't write it off. Remain open-minded but aware. In my opinion, synchronicity is manifestation working effortlessly when we are in harmony with the universe.

Poverty Consciousness

We humans love to put labels on things because it's much easier to file them away in our own minds and over the years and I have heard many people refer to "poverty consciousness". I understand the spiritual relevance of this and that you can use Akashic Record clearings in an attempt to clear "poverty consciousness" from your life, but this alone is not a win-all solution.

You still have to take grounded action to make positive changes in your life. In a physical reality, you have to work actively on all aspects of yourself: Spiritual, emotional, mental, and physical.

Wealth Creation

In the physical, there are 4 important factors of wealth creation are:

- **Income.** You need it to be financially secure and to invest in your future!

- **Saving & Investing.** You need to do it so that you can create passive income, allowing you to become financially independent.

- **Expenses.** Keeping your expenses low creates more disposable income, which you can afford to save more towards your future.

- **Mindset.** As we have explored previously, you need to hold on to money in order to create wealth. Your beliefs can work for and against you.

Your Money Mindset

For the purpose of this book, I will only focus on mindset, as the other factors will involve a deep dive into business planning and cashflow which is outside the scope of this chapter. Financial psychologists believe that we have our own set of money scripts, beliefs, or narratives. These are usually half-truths or unconscious biases passed down to us from our parents and grandparents in our early childhood. These can be phrases we may have heard growing up, such as:

"Money doesn't grow on trees."

"There will NEVER be enough money."

"There will ALWAYS be enough money."

"Having more money will make things better."

"We don't talk about money."

"Money is the root of all evil."

Research from the USA suggests that there are 4 different psychological profiles:

1. **Money Avoidance.** These people repel wealth as their unconscious belief has taken a "vow of poverty" and believe there is nothing good about holding onto money. They never have or talk about money. They may sabotage their own financial success and frequently give money away.

2. **Money Worship.** These people believe the key to happiness is having more and more money. They may carry credit card debt, or overspend on things, because it makes them feel better. People in this category also usually have a lower net wealth. They tend to put work ahead of family.

3. **Money Status.** These people often link their self-worth to their net worth. They may appear to be "wealthy", but they are often over spenders, having come from lower socio-economic backgrounds. They may be guilty of hiding spending from their partner and prone to excessive gambling.

4. **Money Vigilance.** The money vigilant are less likely to have debt and only spend what they can afford. They are smart savers and investors and are in good financial health. They are discreet about their financial status and rarely keep financial secrets from their partner.

Being aware of these archetypes can help us break bad habits and work on the qualities we seek that allow us to have an improved relationship with money.

During our lifetime events in early childhood can also impact our relationship with money; a messy divorce, a business which goes bankrupt, even a financial windfall may affect our lives. Studies from the US suggest that over 70% of lottery winners lose all their money. It has been determined that abrupt shifts in socio-economic status can have a detrimental impact on people's lives. It pushes them away from their communities — their tribe — causing a decline in mental health and wellbeing, which makes them feel "unsafe". Some winners may lose the money due to a lack of financial education. Children who grew up within families that are relatively wealthy inherit some skills and knowledge from their parents and are more likely to keep this wealth as they proceed through life.

If you have a fractured or difficult relationship with money, no level of planning will help you unless you first address your mindset issues; focusing on mindset alone without taking grounded action will not serve to create any form wealth. The trick is to ensure that you are always covering all bases, i.e. balance.

Adjusting To Change

The way my life started in the financial services industry certainly feels like someone else's life and is far removed from where I am today.

The world is evolving for the better and it's our responsibility to recognise this and move with it; either we will, or we won't and when we resist, the universe kicks our arse! Play is so important, don't forget to smile and laugh with friends and family. Get out into nature as much as possible and listen to music; it all helps to raise our vibration.

If you resonate with any of my words or if you have had an abrupt awakening, please take a moment to consider that this is happening for a reason — you are not going mad. Pay attention to images and words; take time to journal, as this will give you valuable insights about yourself. But, don't become consumed or obsessed too much over the detail. Remain in truth and integrity, but respect others' free will and do not impose yours upon them.

Try not to cut and run for the hills as you adjust to the changes and give it time. Who you are at the beginning of this process will evolve and sometimes we come full circle. I believe that we are often divinely positioned, so give yourself time. It is far better to surrender and flow with the current of creation and whilst manifestations can be created in the quantum field, you still need to lay the vibration down onto mother earth by taking grounded actions.

I wish you all the very best of luck with your own journey.

Much love,
Rachael Hall x

Meet Rachael Hall

Rachael Hall is a two-times Global Award Winning Independent Financial Adviser (IFA), CISI Accredited Financial Coach and NHS

Pension Specialist. She provides holistic and bespoke advice for medical professionals, business owners, and entrepreneurs. Rachael is one of the country's leading experts on the UK pension tax system. The Sunday Times, The Financial Times, The Telegraph, and other industry news channels have featured her expertise.

LINKS:

Universal link: https://www.linktr.ee/rachaelhall7

Chapter Nine

Sam Grundy

I am a 44-year-old female Army veteran, mum of two young adults. This is my story.

I have been an activity instructor and a dental nurse. In 2001, I combined the two and joined the Army.

Basic training in the Army was heavily male dominated, with limited variations in physical tests for female soldiers. We all carried the same weight, covered the same distances, and learnt rifle skills. The emphasis was on becoming a soldier first, then being a dental nurse.

I went to Iraq in March 2003, as a dental nurse. We had additional roles on deployment; I was trained in decontamination for chemical warfare. If you can call it lucky by still being in a war zone, they informed us once we had been deployed that our decontamination role wasn't needed. Instead, we then found ourselves fitting into different roles. With my medical background, I helped the team with the disposal of clinical waste. As you can imagine, this came with its own challenges being attached to a field hospital.

My mindset and belief in the world changed.

Navigating Life's Turbulence: Battling Post-Traumatic Stress Disorder (PTSD) and Parenthood

In 2005, I received a medical discharge because of PTSD, fibromyalgia, and other physical conditions. I struggled with what to do with my life and self-sabotage was common.

In 2005, I got married and in 2006 we had a baby girl — life was good. My husband went to Iraq at the end of 2006 and I found out I was pregnant with our son. I struggled mentally whilst he was away, having only been there myself three years previously. I was convinced he would not come home to me. He did! July 2007, we had our son. Life continues. We moved often, being military. I certainly knew how to pack up a house!

Over the space of four years, I had to have some residential therapy for my PTSD; I learnt how to manage it; I had to come to terms with the fact it would never be cured, just managed by using different techniques like mindfulness.

Staying with other veterans going through the same things (but different) as me was an eye opener. On some stays, I was the only female veteran receiving treatment. The camaraderie was there again though, that was a comfort, the dark humour, and banter too.

In 2015, I competed in the Dragonboat Championships as part of a disabled veterans team. We won Bronze. I loved the camaraderie of the team and families. However, because of other physical problems that arose shortly after this, I had to hang up my paddle; I was gutted. I missed it and still do.

Discovering Purpose Amidst Adversity: The Younique Journey

Over the next few years, when the kids were in full-time school and I couldn't do my Dental Nursing anymore, I realised I needed to find something that would help me in the areas that I felt were missing.

I found Younique or should I say it found me! After following some of the other ambassadors for a while, I decided to give it a go.

Although I hit the minimum targets for a few years, my progress in the business didn't really grow. My lack of expertise as a make-up artist or skin care guru made me believe that people wouldn't buy from me.

In August 2022 my marriage of 18yrs broke down. I moved out and stayed with my parents. I felt so low. At a point, I felt like I had nothing, like I was broken and couldn't see a future.

In January 2023, I knew I had to make it my year. I needed to find my purpose and believe in myself again, so I found a new home for me and my children, restarted Younique and decided it was now or never!!

At the end of February, the incentive trip was announced, and I told my daughter that I was going to earn myself a place! It was an all-inclusive cruise in the Bahamas!

The only way I was going to get a place was if I built a team and we worked together.

I got my first team member on the 1st March, which was the first day of the five-month time period. I had to earn points by selling the products and got bonus points by growing my team.

My first thoughts were, what if I don't feel that in myself? How can I promote it to others? But I understood what it meant to have a place to go to, to receive treatment for trauma that wasn't your fault, so that in itself gave me a push in the right direction.

Younique's vision is to uplift, validate and empower others! I needed to feel that in myself before I could promote it to others.

Younique's mission is to help the charity Saprea (formerly The Younique Foundation and Defend Innocence). It is a nonprofit that provides resources to prevent and heal from sexual abuse. Saprea offer retreats and webinars for healing and therapy. Having had to go through residential therapy myself for PTSD, I understand about needing a place to go. That my sales of products were going to help women receive this further fuelled my resolve.

So I set myself a challenge of going live on social media every single day of the incentive time period!

I had the backing of the other ambassadors. They showed me enormous support, no competition amongst us. We are all aiming for the same goal, which is to work with the vision! They helped me behind the scenes by sending messages of support or watching my lives. My confidence grew again. I could see my progress because my team was growing. At the end of the first month, I hit a promotion that I hadn't gained in the previous years.

It gave me the push to go for the next one, which I did in the third month.

By now, my confidence and self-worth had grown. I realised that because I was being honest and open in my live videos about my "new life" that I was creating alongside my PTSD, fibromyalgia, and other conditions. I was showing others that it is ok to have these feelings and still be successful. Everyone is allowed bad days, down days, a little of self-doubt, so long as you don't stay in those feelings.

I realised people were following me and buying from me because I was being honest and my true self. I had also found my sense of humour again. Transformation had happened. My children had seen a difference, too. They were proud of me.

There is no judgement behind the scenes from the other ambassadors. We want everyone to succeed, you just don't get that in the "suit world". There's no competition for the promotions or team growing, we share ideas. I was getting messages from people asking for my advice, which I found strange. I also found it strange when they were telling me I was an inspiration.

I had found a belief in myself again. It was a pleasant feeling, so I shared it more on social media during month four and five. End of month five went crazy, it was close to the end of the incentive trip qualification period and I still had a way to go, but with some hard work, others joining my team and the continued support from the wider network of women I earned a place on the trip!

From Survivor to Mentor: Embracing Mindfulness and Personal Growth

With the help of Younique's vision of uplifting, validating and empowering women, it helped me to see what I already had inside me, that it had been hidden away for too long, and all because of the "imposter imp" that sat on my shoulder telling me I couldn't do it, that I wasn't confident enough to do it, or have the background to back it up.

Well, I found out that I had all that because I will learn from others, to not compete with anyone other than my own thoughts!

I had to start with myself before I could start helping others.

This has now also led onto to me working towards qualifications in mindfulness and life coaching. I've realised that my purpose for this next part of my life is to help people. More specifically, to help others find their inner strength, to grow into the people they are.

What Is Mindfulness?

Simply, it is "living in the present moment". It means being intentionally more aware and awake to your surroundings. There are both mental and physical benefits to practising mindfulness.

Box breathing is great for beginners. If you practise this at your calmest times, it will then be very beneficial in a more stressful moment or even during a bit of a panic time.

Find a space where you can sit comfortably. If possible, take off your socks and shoes so you can feel the ground under your feet. This is a great grounding practice too. You can close your eyes or keep them open, whichever makes you more comfortable.

Imagine a four-sided box in front of you. You will start in one corner and trace it whilst you breathe in and out.

1.   Up the first side, you breathe in for the count of three seconds.

2.   Across the top, you hold your breath for the count of three seconds.

3.   Down the side, you breathe in for the count of three seconds.

4.   Across the bottom, you hold your breath for the count of three seconds.

5.   Repeat.

You can repeat this as many times as you like until you feel calm. It is also a good one to do if you struggle to fall asleep at night.

When Did Mindfulness Find Its Way into My Life?

One of my first experiences of mindfulness was when I had several residential therapy stays with Combat Stress to help with my PTSD. It was timetabled, so I had to attend the sessions. I thought it was going to be rubbish and pointless … how wrong was I?

I learnt that mindfulness can be done many ways, from breathing techniques, body scans, to simple games like eye spy.

The way mindfulness is most effective is by being grounded first. It's one of the first things I explain to people. Being grounded keeps you in the here and now. So, I ask people to take off their socks and shoes (*unless driving!*) so they can feel the ground below their feet; notice the texture and temperature.

The body scan is a particular favourite of mine. Having physical and mental issues, it covers all bases. It starts on your toes and goes to your head, tensing each part for a couple of seconds before then releasing it.

My other favourite is Monkey Mind. This technique is great for overthinkers, people that catastrophise or have intrusive thoughts … or, like me, all the above!

Monkey Mind is great for those thoughts that are just not needed until you are ready to deal with them. It is linked with Buddhist principles and refers to being unsettled, restless or even confusion.

I like to use this practice for my intrusive or unhelpful thoughts.

Monkey Mind insists on being heard. It takes a lot of self-control to shut it down. It is part of the brain that becomes easily distracted.

When I first heard about this, I instantly imagined a monkey!

So it then became my brain mascot!

For every intrusive, unhelpful, or negative thought, I turn them into monkeys.

I acknowledge the monkey (*thought*) and thank it for turning up. I tell it I'm not needing it right now. Then, I give it a banana and tell Monkey to sit in the tree and eat it whilst I finish the task that is more important.

If you haven't finished the task and the monkey thought returns … give it a bigger banana!

When I've explained this to people and they try it, the response is good. In fact, they have told me it actually makes them smile because of the humour attached to it.

Vision boards have helped my journey too, and it was easier than I thought it would be to get started. I just got a giant piece of paper and in the centre I wrote my time frame 2023-2024. Then I turned it into a good old spider gram. I initially put on buzz words about what I want to work on, i.e. self-confidence, self-worth, targets that I saw in Younique for promotions and events.

It's now made me believe in the law of attraction, every single thing that I have put on my vision board, whether it's a buzzword or an actual target has been ticked off … a couple of them earlier than the date I put next to it!

The vision board is only a small part of the whole. Underneath that is the self-care and mindfulness. I feel though these come in hand-in-hand with one another.

Get yourself a good skin care routine and some quiet time in a morning really sets you up for the day ahead.

Box breathing, body scans, grounding are all great mindfulness practices. By practising these techniques when you're calm, it becomes easier to use them during those times of need. For example, when a panic attack strikes or (*in my case*) when you experience flashbacks and nightmares.

What Does Fibromyalgia Mean To Me?

Fibromyalgia is not a one size fits all kind of illness. It affects people in different ways.

For me, and the way I explain to my children and family is if you imagine one of the worst bruises you have had...that's my body ALL over! I feel fatigued, which then makes me snappy and irritable. On my worst days, even wearing clothes hurts.

It affects stress levels in your body, the weather can affect you too, winter is the worst for me.

I also have "brain-fog" which means it affects my cognitive behaviour, trouble remembering, concentration and attention....which made writing this chapter of the book really challenging!

There are so many symptoms that I could write about but the above are the more relevant.

Mindfulness helps with most of my symptoms, but I do still struggle...but it doesn't define who I am or stop me from achieving things. It just means I do it a lot slower than others.

Lady gaga has fibromyalgia, as does Morgan Freeman, and they are *famous*! They still achieve their goals and roles, they just know how to pace themselves. Lady Gaga revealed in her documentary "five foot two" that she lives with chronic pain. Morgan Freeman still wears a compression glove on his hand, he explained in Esquire in 2012 that it was from an accident that causes shooting pain up and down his arm.

Self-care is another important thing I practice, although some days it is hard to keep up with it, especially if I'm in a flare.

Self-care can mean so many things. Examples of self-care activities are washing/bathing, reading, limiting screen time, personal growth, and mindfulness.

Personal development is activities that develop your capabilities and potential. There are five areas that you can explore: mentally, spiritually, socially, physically and emotionally.

Develop new skills and find motivation by taking action and surrounding yourself with a supportive network. This is where a vision board will help. It will help you set achievable goals in both personal and professional areas of your life.

Absolutely everything I have written about has helped with my PTSD in one way or another.

It's like a jigsaw puzzle where you don't actually know the finished picture, mainly because nobody has ever assembled it before. You think it's going to be the picture of you before you were told you had PTSD, but it's not. That person has gone, changed, turned into a new person.

Having PTSD for so long and not having a cure for it, just self-management, means it's been a journey of self-discovery. Learning how to live every day with something inside your head and not knowing if it's going to explode or stay dormant. It has been necessary for me to learn about my triggers and how they will affect my daily routine and family. Some days I struggle with the most basic of functions, like washing my face! This is because of the PTSD and depression combined with fibromyalgia. Yep, I truly am a good mix of things!

But, I am inspired by the Royal family's involvement with the charity Mind™. I too want to raise awareness of mental health.

Sharing the education behind it is important, so that family and loved ones know how to help and cope with any situation or triggered episode that happens.

PTSD has affected me in every aspect of my life and my family. Which is why doing all the things I've written about has been important to me. I'm on a journey and the final destination is still unknown. But for the first time in a long time, I'm enjoying seeing the twists and turns in the road ahead. By avoiding self-sabotage behaviour and letting self-doubt creep in, I know I will find my final destination – wherever that is. By sharing my journey, I'm hoping that I can help others find their inner sparkle again ... just like I have!

The Wellness Workshop: Sharing Tools for Emotional Resilience and Self-Care

I had the idea I had to help others, not just veterans, but other Younique ambassadors, men, women, and children!

I had been chatting with friends for a while about the different techniques we had used in similar situations in our lives. One friend was an expert about journalling, another was a true crystal guru, whilst I know all about grounding and mindfulness. I did a few joint lives with some of my friends on a Facebook page I set up; it became popular and a name was chosen ... The Wellness Workshop was born!

Every Wednesday I do wellness walks and a Wellness Wednesday live. The subjects range from journalling and how it can help with emotions, why we react different ways in the moon cycles, how we can help clear out unhelpful thoughts, and useful mindfulness techniques.

I have a big vision of branching off Facebook and go into my local community to do some face-to-face sessions in a little "pop up" room. Eventually, I'd love to have my own premises with the business name on a banner.

I firmly believe in the law of attraction and positive mindset. I have shared our vision and determination with the universe. Stay tuned.

The Wellness Workshop is not a one size fits all programme. I chat about the different practices on offer and spend time with my members to tailor make it for their needs.

If you are not a member, like and follow our Facebook page to watch the Wellness Wednesday lives. Even these short live videos have had some great feedback. One lady thanked me for the help one of our lives did for her and her children. The journalling and mindfulness connected to give her activities to help her children explain some worries they had in their heads.

Sometimes talking isn't helpful because you cannot always find the right words. But journalling is different. You are writing to an imaginary person, or drawing a picture that shows frustration as squiggles. It then becomes mindfulness when you colour in between the lines.

I work out how many sessions you may need, and provide you with some worksheets to do in between the sessions that help with the continuity and reflection.

Benefits of Mindfulness Sessions.

Mindfulness helps with you understanding your emotions and cope better with difficult thoughts. You feel calmer and can boost your attention and concentration on the here and now.

Studies show that mindfulness can help with stress, anxiety, and depression.

It helps us to pay attention to what is happening inside and outside of ourselves. You can easily get caught in your thoughts without stopping to notice how those thoughts are driving your behaviour and emotions.

Mindfulness helps you to reconnect with your body by using your senses. Paying more attention to the smells, sounds, sights, tastes of that present moment. It could be something as simple as using the touch of the texture of the clothes you are wearing.

When we become more aware of the here and now, we experience things we have taken for granted. It increases our awareness of unhelpful thought patterns.

Researchers have found a link between mindfulness at work and higher job satisfaction, as well as reduced emotional exhaustion. It helps with stress resilience, increased focus, and increased productivity.

A key part of The Wellness Workshop is access to a variety of techniques. For example, I pair a mindfulness practice with journal prompts during our twelve-week programme.

What is Journalling?

Journalling is a powerful tool. It is the technique of writing about your thoughts, feelings, and sensations as they come up in your day-to-day life. My journalling workbook explains how to journal and what to journal, so you can make the most of this type of writing. There are at least twelve types of ways to journal; we have created a booklet that explains these for you. My advice would be to try them all and then decide what suits your needs.

The Wellness Workshop has helped many overcome and come to terms with their own emotions. The aim of The Wellness Workshop is to give you the tools you need to be able to cope with stress, anxiety, and any trauma you may encounter. Having the coping mechanism in place can prevent these emotions from escalating any further.

It's important to make sure you choose the journalling method you want to practise, gather your tools which are as simple as pen and paper. It's equally important that you find the right space to journal. This needs to be a safe environment where you can express your emotions. You do not want to be looking over your shoulders whilst writing.

Some people don't think the timing of journalling can make a difference, but this is a significant factor in journalling for many reasons. You may feel you need to journal first thing in the morning to help you feel more positive about the day and give you that boost you need. Or you may prefer to journal before bed as you need to release the tension you have been carrying all day. Whatever you need, remember it's your tool box and you personalise it to suit your needs.

Get comfortable and start journalling. How you feel will surprise you. Snuggle with your favourite blanket, a cup of tea and some candles or music on in the background. Whatever you decide to go with it and enjoy.

The twelve ways to journal that we use in our workshops are:

- ☐ Reflection Journal

- ☐ Journalling with Prompts

- ☐ Letter writing journalling

- ☐ Gratitude journalling

- ☐ Journalling with Visual Prompts

- ☐ Bullet journalling

- ☐ Sketchbook or Scrapbook journalling

- ☐ Dream journalling

- ☐ Free writing

- ☐ Planning and goal journal

- ☐ Digital journal

- ☐ Audio journal

Members in the group asked what they should do with their journal once the twelve weeks ends. It is advisable to keep the journal and revisit it after three, six, or twelve months. It's a powerful tool as you progress in your personal development. You may not think you have come on from day-to-day but actually taking time to read a journal from as little as three months ago is magic.

The Wellness Workshop is a project that is constantly improving. We offer various mindfulness and wellbeing sessions for everyone to benefit from. Our workshops are not just for adults, we also work with children and have created a workbook for them. Journalling is a fantastic resource to use for children who struggle to express their emotions. Using the Journal methods along with the mindfulness techniques creates a solid foundation for success.

Meet Sam Grundy

Samantha is a 44-year-old female Army veteran, devoted mother of two young adults, and a resilient soul on a journey of self-discovery and empowerment. Her path, marked by both adversity and triumph, reflects her unwavering commitment to personal growth and holistic healing.

After serving as an activity instructor and dental nurse, Samantha's life took a transformative turn in 2001 when she joined the Army. Her experiences in the military, including deployment to Iraq as a dental nurse amidst the chaos of war, profoundly reshaped her worldview and instilled in her a newfound resilience.

In 2005, Samantha faced the daunting challenge of a medical discharge due to PTSD, fibromyalgia, and other physical conditions. Despite the setbacks, she found solace in motherhood and embarked on a journey of self-healing and self-discovery.

Samantha's resilience and determination shone through as she navigated the complexities of PTSD, marital struggles, and physical ailments. Through introspection and perseverance, she emerged stronger, determined to carve out a purpose-driven life.

In 2023, Samantha embarked on a new chapter, reigniting her passion for personal development and mindfulness as a Younique ambassador. Through her journey with Younique, Samantha discovered the power of self-belief and authenticity, inspiring others to embrace their inner strength and pursue their dreams.

Today, Samantha is a beacon of hope and positivity, dedicated to uplifting and empowering others through her work with The Wellness Workshop. Alongside her friends, Samantha shares tools for emotional resilience, self-care, and mindfulness, guiding individuals on a transformative journey toward holistic wellbeing.

As a certified mindfulness practitioner and aspiring life coach, Samantha continues to champion mental health awareness and personal growth, believing that every individual possesses the inner resilience to overcome life's challenges and thrive.

LINKS

Facebook: https://www.facebook.com/TheWellnessWorkshop24

9 781068 678301